Volume equivalents

METRIC	IMPERIAL	METRIC	IMPERIAL
30ml	1fl oz	450ml	15fl oz
60ml	2fl oz	500ml	16fl oz
75ml	2½fl oz	600ml	1 pint
100ml	3½fl oz	750ml	1¼ pints
120ml	4fl oz	900ml	1½ pints
150ml	5fl oz (¼ pint)	1 litre	1¾ pints
175ml	6fl oz	1.2 litres	2 pints
200ml	7fl oz (⅓ pint)	1.4 litres	2½ pints
240ml	8fl oz	1.5 litres	2¾ pints
300ml	10fl oz (½ pint)	1.7 litres	3 pints
350ml	12fl oz	2 litres	3½ pints
400ml	14fl oz	3 litres	5¼ pints

D0319840

Weight equivalents

METRIC	IMPERIAL	METRIC	IMPERIAL
15g	½oz	150g	5½oz
20g	¾oz	175g	6oz
25g	scant 1oz	200g	7oz
30g	1oz	225g	8oz
45g	1½oz	250g	9oz
50g	1¾oz	300g	10oz
60g	2oz	450g	1lb
75g	2½oz	500g	1lb 2oz
85g	3oz	675g	1½lb
100g	3½oz	900g	2lb
115g	4oz	1kg	2¼lb
125g	4½oz	1.5kg	3lb 3oz
140g	5oz	1.8kg	4lb

SCOTTISH BORDERS LIBRARY SERVICES	
008341634	
Bertrams	02/12/2010
641.615	£12.99

everyday easy

Dinner in the Freezer

hearty soups • casseroles • curries
oven bakes • savoury tarts

DK

LONDON, NEW YORK, MELBOURNE,
MUNICH, AND DELHI

Editor Shashwati Tia Sarkar
Project Art Editors Elly King, Kathryn Wilding
Senior Jackets Creative Nicola Powling
Managing Editor Dawn Henderson
Managing Art Editor Marianne Markham
Senior Production Editor Jennifer Murray
Production Controller Poppy Newdick

DK INDIA

Editorial Manager Glenda Fernandes
Designer Neha Ahuja
Editor Alicia Ingty
Assistant Designer Nidhi Mehra
Assistant Editor Megha Gupta
DTP Co-ordinator Sunil Sharma
DTP Operator Saurabh Challariya

Material first published in *The Cooking Book*, 2008
and *Cook Express*, 2009

This edition first published in Great Britain in 2010
by Dorling Kindersley Limited
80 Strand, London WC2R 0RL

A Penguin Company

Copyright © 2008, 2009, 2010 Dorling Kindersley
Text copyright © 2008, 2009, 2010 Dorling Kindersley

2 4 6 8 10 9 7 5 3 1

All rights reserved. No part of this publication
may be reproduced, stored in a retrieval system,
or transmitted in any form or by any means,
electronic, mechanical, photocopying,
recording, or otherwise without the prior
written permission of the copyright owners.
A CIP catalogue record for this book
is available from the British Library.

ISBN 978-1-4053-5645-9

Printed and bound in Singapore by Tien Wah Press

Discover more at
www.dk.com

CONTENTS

SCOTTISH BORDERS COUNCIL

LIBRARY &

INFORMATION SERVICES

Batch and freeze

Double your cooking one night and freeze half for easy batch cooking, or cook for the freezer if you have time. Always cool food completely before freezing and thaw slowly; it is safer and will help retain the food's flavour and texture.

FOOD	PACKAGING	STORAGE	DEFROST
SOUPS AND STOCKS Once cooked, leave to cool completely, then pack into portions as needed. Don't freeze in over-large portions, as defrosting will take too long.	Pack in sealable plastic containers or freezer bags. The liquid will expand a little, so leave room for this. Stocks can be spooned into ice cube trays; once frozen, remove from the tray and transfer to a freezer bag and seal.	Soups for up to 3 months. Stocks for up to 6 months.	Thaw overnight in the refrigerator, then reheat in a pan until piping hot, or heat in the microwave on High for a few minutes.
SAUCES These take up little space in the freezer. If sauces call for the addition of egg yolk or cream, omit and add later. Cool completely before freezing.	Freeze in sealable freezerproof containers, bags, or ice cube trays. If using ice cube trays, once frozen, remove from the tray, transfer to a freezer bag, and seal. Leave air space for expansion.	Up to 3 months.	Thaw overnight in the refrigerator, then reheat in a pan until piping hot, or heat in the microwave on High for a few minutes.
CASSEROLES AND CURRIES Fatty meats can go rancid after a while in the freezer, so choose lean cuts. When doubling up recipes, be careful not to over season; $1^{1}/_{2}$ times the usual is often enough.	Freeze in sealable freezer bags or foil containers, or ladle into rigid sealable plastic containers. Make sure meat is well covered with liquid, otherwise it will dry out.	Up to 3 months.	Thaw overnight in the refrigerator, then reheat in a pan until piping hot, or heat in the microwave on High for a few minutes. Take extra care that the meat is really hot before serving and do not reheat more than once.
PIES AND TARTS Baking is the ideal time to batch cook. You can freeze pastry cooked or uncooked. Cool completely before freezing.	**Uncooked:** Freeze blocks of pastry layered with greaseproof paper, then wrapped in cling film. **Cooked:** Freeze pies and tarts wrapped in greaseproof paper followed by a double layer of cling film.	Uncooked pies and pastry for up to 3 months. Cooked pies and pastry cases for up to 6 months.	Bake uncooked tart shells and pastries from frozen in the oven at 200°C (400°F) for 15 minutes. Thaw cooked pies and tarts overnight in the refrigerator, then bake at 180°C (350°F), for about 30 minutes, or until piping hot.

Tips for freezing

Follow these guidelines to prevent loss of quality, texture, taste, colour, or nutrients, but never re-freeze anything that has been frozen before – there is a high risk of bacteria multiplying in the thawing process before re-freezing.

The fresher the food is when it goes in the freezer, the better it will be when it comes out. If you are aware of this when planning your shopping and cooking you'll preserve the quality of the food.

Plan ahead when making big batches (doubling or tripling your recipe) as most dishes only freeze for up to 3 months, and you don't want too much of one dish.

Package the food in sensible amounts to prevent wastage – you should not re-freeze after thawing. For soups, allow about 300ml (10fl oz) per person; avoid portion sizes larger than 600ml (1 pint). Try freezing in different portion sizes, too, to suit your requirements – larger portions for family meals and portions-for-one for when you are home alone and don't want to cook.

Label your containers so you know what is what and how long it has been frozen for. You could also use coloured bags or boxes and develop a coding system for yourself.

To save space, once foods are frozen, they can be removed from their solid container and re-packed tightly in foil, cling film, or resealable freezer bags. Foods will freeze quicker if you leave plenty of room around them or store them in the bottom of the freezer, where it is coldest.

Remember to rotate things in the freezer so everything gets used in time. It's first in, first out!

Avoid freezing...

Cream cheese or cottage cheese will separate or become watery, as will cream, unless it has been lightly whipped first.

Mayonnaise and hollandaise sauce will also separate when they are defrosted.

Fatty foods become fattier, and eventually turn rancid.

Salad ingredients such as cucumber, lettuce, celery, and tomatoes turn to water once defrosted.

If you are unsure whether something will freeze, test a small amount first.

Once frozen, ice cubes should be re-packaged in a sealable container to prevent freezer burn.

Freezer packaging

The right packaging will protect your food so it keeps for longer. Remember to label each package, including portions sizes and packing and expiry dates.

PACKAGING	BEST FOR	HOW TO USE
PLASTIC CONTAINERS Use ones that are durable so they don't become brittle and crack at low temperatures. They are available in all shapes and sizes and are easy to label and reuse.	Rigid plastic containers can be used to freeze all types of foods. They are especially good for bulky dishes that include a lot of sauce, such as casseroles, stews, and curries.	Leave the food to cool before filling the container and freezing. The plastic container can be placed in the refrigerator when it is time to defrost.
ICE CUBE TRAYS Freezing sauces and stocks in small portions allows you to make a large batch that you can use over time.	Ideal for freezing small amounts of sauce or stock. You could also use them to freeze leftover red wine, which you can then add to gravies or sauces.	Carefully fill with the liquid, leaving a little room for it to expand. Freeze when completely cool. Once frozen, transfer the cubes to plastic freezer bags or plastic containers and seal (otherwise the food will get freezer burn).
FOIL DISHES These are a good choice if freezing foods for a few months. Use heavy-duty aluminium ones.	Most types of food can be frozen in foil dishes, but they are particularly useful for oven bakes because they are both ovenproof and freezerproof.	You can cook, freeze, and reheat foil trays in the oven. They can be recycled, but not the lids, as these are cardboard.
FOIL Foil can be used to create your own container, especially if you have a limited collection of ovenware.	This is best for recipes that you can cook in the oven, including lasagnes, potato-topped pies, gratins, and roasts.	Double-line an ovenproof dish with foil, then fill with the food for cooking. Cook as per the recipe, leave to cool, then freeze. Once frozen, lift out the foil dish and either wrap well in plastic wrap, or cover with a large freezer bag. Seal, and return to the freezer.

PACKAGING		BEST FOR	HOW TO USE
	BAGS FOR LIQUID You can store liquids in plastic bags by freezing them first in a rigid plastic container. This is an excellent way of saving containers and space.	Soups, sauces, ragùs, curries, and stews.	Line a plastic container with a freezerproof bag, then fill with stock, soup, or sauce and seal well with clips, leaving some room for the contents to expand. Freeze until solid, then remove the container and stack the solid bag.
	PLASTIC FREEZER BAGS Freezer bags are very versatile for freezing. They need to be strong, leakproof, and resistant to moisture.	Most foods can be stored in polythene freezer bags. Bags with a built-in seal are ideal for sauces, stews, and blanched vegetables.	Allow the food to cool completely before packing it in a freezer bag and storing in the freezer.

A guide to symbols

The recipes in this book are accompanied by symbols that alert you to important information.

 Tells you how many people the recipe serves, or how much is produced.

Indicates how much time you will need to prepare and cook a dish. Next to this symbol you will also find out if additional time is required for such things as marinating, standing, proving, or chilling. Read the recipe to find out exactly how much extra time to allow.

Points out a healthy dish – low in fat or has a low GI (Glycaemic Index).

This is especially important, as it alerts you to what has to be done before you can begin to cook the recipe. For example, you may need to soak some beans overnight.

 This denotes that special equipment is required, such as a deep-fat fryer or skewers. Where possible, alternatives are given.

RECIPE CHOOSERS

Spicy

Chilli beef and bean soup
page 36

Chicken and chilli burgers
page 120

Chicken korma page 66

Curried vegetable pies
page 186

Vegetable curry page 52

Garlic and chilli chicken with honey sweet potato page 74

Stuffed aubergines page 128

Chilli con carne page 94

Pan-fried lamb with green chillies page 118

Thai crab cakes page 126

Chickpea curry with cardamom page 58

Black bean and coconut soup page 40

Chicken jalfrezi page 72

Couscous royale page 50

Caribbean stew with allspice and ginger page 64

Spicy beef pies page 170

13

Comfort

Split pea and bacon soup
page 38

Lamb and pea pie page 176

Beef ragù page 194

Shepherd's pie page 140

Beef and celeriac casserole with stout and anchovies page 88

Chicken and sweetcorn pie page 174

Fish and leek pie page 178

Sausages with butter beans page 100

Moussaka page 136

Leek and potato soup page 28

Haddock mornay page 152

Cheese and onion pie page 182

Cheesy potato and mushroom gratin page 146

Chicken and cornmeal cobbler page 70

Pork with rice and tomatoes page 84

Healthy

Mixed bean medley page 48

Lamb daube page 82

Thick vegetable soup page 32

Chunky ratatouille page 54

Pork and bean casserole
page 90

Shepherdless pie page 150

**Garlic and chilli chicken with
honey sweet potato** page 74

**Lamb, spinach, and chickpea
hotpot** page 102

Braised turkey with vegetables page 60

Vegetarian moussaka
page 148

Chicken and chilli burgers
page 120

Bean and rosemary soup
page 30

Chickpea curry with cardamom
page 58

**Pearl barley and borlotti bean
one-pot** page 56

Mixed fish kebabs page 116

Great for a crowd

Lamb and aubergine ragù
page 196

Lamb daube page 82

Game stew page 104

Shin of beef with Marsala
page 76

Pork with fennel and mustard
page 78

Spiced sausage cassoulet
page 96

Beef stew with orange and bay leaves page 98

Spanish meatballs page 110

Vegetarian leek and mushroom lasagne page 142

Pork goulash page 80

Chilli con carne page 94

Pork and bean casserole
page 90

Beef and celeriac casserole with stout and anchovies page 88

Chicken and cornmeal cobbler
page 70

Vegetarian

Cheesy potato and mushroom gratin page 146

Mixed mushroom and walnut tart page 190

Calzone with peppers, capers, and olives page 166

Red lentil and tomato soup page 26

Shepherdless pie page 150

Vegetarian moussaka page 148

Stuffed aubergines page 128

Aubergine parmigiana page 134

Gruyère, potato, and thyme tartlets page 188

Chunky ratatouille page 54

Vegetarian leek and mushroom lasagne page 142

Thick vegetable soup page 32

Vegetable curry page 52

Swiss chard and Gruyère cheese tart page 168

Mushroom and ricotta pies with red pepper pesto page 184

Pearl barley and borlotti bean one-pot page 56

Make vegetable stock

Stocks can be made in large quantities and then frozen for up to 6 months. They are invaluable ingredients for soups, risottos, casseroles, and more.

1 Place chopped carrots, celery, onion and a bouquet garni into a large stockpot. Cover with water and bring to the boil. Reduce the heat and simmer the stock for up to 1 hour.

2 Ladle through a fine sieve, pressing the vegetables against the sieve to extract any extra liquid. Season to taste with salt and freshly ground black pepper. Let cool and refrigerate for up to 3 days, or freeze.

Make chicken stock

Simmering the remains of your roast chicken with a few vegetables and herbs will produce a light golden stock that you can freeze for up to 6 months.

1 Add either raw chicken bones, the whole carcass, or the bones and scraps from a cooked chicken into a large stockpot with carrots, celery, onions, and a bouquet garni of fresh herbs.

2 Cover with water and bring to the boil. Reduce the heat and simmer for 2–3 hours, skimming frequently. Ladle through a fine sieve and season. Let cool and refrigerate for up to 3 days, or freeze.

Make beef stock

Using beef bones will produce a richer and darker stock than chicken, particularly if you roast the bones first. Freeze the stock for up to 6 months.

1 Use either leftover bones from a rib of roast beef, or ask your butcher for a bag of beef bones. Tip the bones into a large roasting tin, add a handful of vegetables such as carrot tops, celery chunks, onion pieces and skin, and season. Roast for 30 minutes.

2 Add the roasted bones and vegetables to a large deep pan with some fresh stalks of thyme, rosemary, or a woody herb of your choice, then pour over enough cold water to cover the contents of the pan completely.

3 Bring to the boil, then reduce to a gentle simmer. Cook with the lid half-on for about 1 hour, skimming any skum that comes to the top of the pan, if necessary.

4 Remove the bones from the pan and discard, then strain the liquid through a fine sieve into a large storage container, and season to taste. Let cool and refrigerate for up to 2 days, or freeze.

Red lentil and tomato soup

With a hint of chilli, this is a thick, warming soup.

INGREDIENTS

2 tbsp olive oil
2 onions, finely chopped
4 garlic cloves, grated or finely chopped
pinch of chilli flakes
4 carrots, finely chopped
salt and freshly ground black pepper
450g (1lb) red lentils
3 x 400g cans chopped tomatoes
1.4 litres (2^1/$_2$ pints) hot vegetable stock

METHOD

1 Heat the oil in a large pan, add the onions, and cook over a low heat for 6–8 minutes, or until soft and translucent. Stir through the garlic, chilli flakes, and carrots, season with salt and pepper, and cook for 2 minutes.

2 Add the lentils, stir, then add the tomatoes and stock. Bring to the boil, then simmer on a very low heat for 35–40 minutes, or until the lentils are soft. Transfer to a blender or food processor and whiz until blended and smooth. Taste, and season with salt and pepper if needed.

FREEZING INSTRUCTIONS Leave the soup to cool completely, then freeze in a sealable freezerproof container for up to 3 months. To serve, defrost in the refrigerator overnight, then reheat gently in a pan until piping hot.

GOOD WITH Fresh crusty bread.

serves 8

**prep 15 mins
• cook 50 mins**

healthy option

**blender or
food processor**

Leek and potato soup

Potatoes give this homely soup body, while leeks lend a silky texture.

INGREDIENTS
2 tbsp olive oil
2 onions, finely chopped
salt and freshly ground black pepper
3 garlic cloves, grated or finely chopped
6 sage leaves, finely chopped
900g (2lb) leeks, cleaned and finely sliced
1.4 litres (2½ pints) hot vegetable stock
900g (2lb) potatoes, peeled and roughly chopped
150ml (5fl oz) double cream, to serve

METHOD

1 Heat the oil in a large pan, add the onions, and cook over a low heat for 6–8 minutes, or until soft and translucent. Season with salt and pepper, then stir in the garlic and sage. Add the leeks and stir well, then cook over a low heat for 10 minutes, or until the leeks are starting to soften.

2 Pour in the stock, bring to the boil, then add the potatoes and simmer for 20 minutes, or until soft. Transfer to a blender or food processor and whiz until blended and smooth. Taste, and season with salt and pepper if needed. Return to the pan to reheat gently, then stir through the cream to serve.

FREEZING INSTRUCTIONS Omit the cream if freezing as it may separate. Leave the soup to cool completely, then freeze in a sealable freezerproof container for up to 3 months. To serve, defrost in the refrigerator overnight, then reheat gently in a pan, stir in the cream when almost hot, and heat through until piping hot.

GOOD WITH Fresh crusty bread.

serves 8

**prep 15 mins
• cook 40 mins**

**blender or
food processor**

Bean and rosemary soup

Simple, hearty soups like this one are great to have on stand-by in the freezer.

INGREDIENTS
2 tbsp olive oil, plus a little extra (according to taste)
2 onions, finely chopped
salt and freshly ground black pepper
1 tbsp rosemary leaves, finely chopped
a few sage leaves, finely chopped
4 celery sticks, finely chopped
3 garlic cloves, grated or finely chopped
2 tbsp tomato purée
2 x 400g cans cannellini beans, drained and rinsed
1.2 litres (2 pints) hot chicken stock
2.5kg (5$\frac{1}{2}$lb) potatoes, cut into chunky pieces

METHOD
1 Heat the oil in a large pan, add the onions, and cook over a low heat for 6–8 minutes, or until soft and translucent. Season well with salt and pepper, then stir in the rosemary, sage, celery, and garlic, and cook over a very low heat, stirring occasionally, for 10 minutes.

2 Stir through the tomato purée and beans, add a little more olive oil if you wish, and cook gently for 5 minutes. Pour in the stock, bring to the boil, then add the potatoes and simmer gently for 15 minutes, or until cooked. Taste, and season again with salt and pepper if needed. Add a little hot stock if the soup is too thick.

FREEZING INSTRUCTIONS Leave the soup to cool completely, then freeze in a sealable freezerproof container for up to 3 months. To serve, defrost in the refrigerator overnight, then reheat gently in a saucepan until piping hot. Add a little hot water or hot stock if the soup is too thick. Alternatively, reheat in a microwave on Medium for 2–3 minutes, then stir and heat for a further 2–3 minutes until piping hot. Leave the soup to stand for 5 minutes before serving.

GOOD WITH Fresh crusty bread.

serves 8

prep 15 mins
• cook 40 mins

healthy option

Thick vegetable soup

This chunky soup is a good winter warmer.

INGREDIENTS
2 tbsp olive oil
2 onions, finely chopped
salt and freshly ground black pepper
4 garlic cloves, grated or finely chopped
1 tbsp rosemary leaves, finely chopped
4 celery sticks, finely chopped
4 carrots, finely chopped
4 courgettes, finely chopped
2 x 400g cans whole tomatoes, chopped in the can
1.2 litres (2 pints) hot vegetable stock
handful of flat-leaf parsley, finely chopped

METHOD
1 Heat the oil in a large pan, add the onions, and cook over a low heat for 6–8 minutes, or until soft and translucent. Season with salt and pepper, then add the garlic, rosemary, celery, and carrots, and cook over a low heat, stirring occasionally, for 10 minutes.

2 Add the courgettes and cook for 5 minutes, then stir in the tomatoes, and squash with the back of a fork. Add the stock, bring to the boil, then reduce to a simmer and cook for 20 minutes. Season well with salt and pepper, then stir through the parsley.

FREEZING INSTRUCTIONS Leave the soup to cool completely, then freeze in a sealable freezerproof container for up to 3 months. To serve, defrost in the refrigerator overnight, then reheat gently in a saucepan until piping hot. Add a little hot water or hot stock if the soup is too thick. Alternatively, reheat in a microwave on Medium for 2–3 minutes, then stir and heat for a further 2–3 minutes until piping hot. Leave the soup to stand for 5 minutes before serving.

GOOD WITH Fresh crusty bread.

serves 8

prep 15 mins
• cook 45 mins

healthy option

Chestnut and bacon soup

The crunchy texture and nutty flavour of this soup is very satisfying.

INGREDIENTS

2 tbsp olive oil
2 onions, finely chopped
250g (9oz) bacon or pancetta, chopped into bite-sized pieces
4 garlic cloves, grated or finely chopped
1 tbsp rosemary leaves, finely chopped
salt and freshly ground black pepper
3 x 200g packets ready-cooked chestnuts, chopped
1.2 litres (2 pints) hot chicken stock
extra virgin olive oil, to serve

METHOD

1 Heat the oil in a large pan, add the onions, and cook over a low heat for 5–8 minutes, or until soft and translucent. Add the bacon or pancetta and cook for 5 minutes, or until crispy. Stir in the garlic and rosemary, then season well with salt and pepper.

2 Stir in the chestnuts, pour in the stock, and bring to the boil. Lower the heat and simmer for 15–20 minutes. Using a slotted spoon, remove a couple of spoonfuls of the bacon and put to one side. Transfer the rest of the soup to a blender or food processor and whiz until puréed.

3 Transfer back to the pan, taste and season again with salt and pepper if needed, then add the reserved bacon pieces. Add a little hot water if the soup is too thick. Serve with a drizzle of extra virgin olive oil.

FREEZING INSTRUCTIONS Leave the soup to cool completely, then transfer to a sealable freezerproof container, making sure the bacon pieces are covered by liquid. Freeze for up to 3 months. To serve, defrost overnight in the refrigerator, then reheat gently in a saucepan until piping hot. Add a little hot water if the soup is too thick. Alternatively, reheat in a microwave on Medium for 2–3 minutes, then stir and heat for a further 2–3 minutes until piping hot. Leave the soup to stand for 5 minutes. Serve with a drizzle of extra virgin olive oil.

GOOD WITH Fresh crusty bread.

serves 8

prep 15 mins
• cook 30 mins

blender or
food processor

Chilli beef and bean soup

Spicy Tex-Mex-style flavours are sure to make this soup a favourite.

INGREDIENTS

2 tbsp olive oil
2 onions, finely chopped
salt and freshly ground black pepper
2 red peppers, deseeded and finely chopped
2–3 red chillies, deseeded and finely chopped
550g (1¼lb) braising steak, cut into 2.5cm (1in) cubes
1 tbsp plain flour
2.3 litres (4 pints) hot beef stock
2 x 400g cans kidney beans, drained, rinsed, and drained again
handful of flat-leaf parsley, finely chopped, to serve

METHOD

1 Heat the oil in a large heavy-based pan, add the onions, and cook on a low heat for 6–8 minutes, or until soft and translucent. Season with salt and pepper, then stir through the red peppers and chillies and cook for 5 minutes. Add the meat and cook, stirring frequently, for 5–10 minutes, or until beginning to brown all over.

2 Sprinkle in the flour, stir well, and cook for 2 minutes. Add the stock, bring to the boil, then cover with a lid and reduce to a simmer. Cook for 1 hour 30 minutes, or until the meat is tender. Add the kidney beans and cook for 10 minutes more, then season to taste with salt and pepper. Stir through the parsley, and serve.

FREEZING INSTRUCTIONS Leave the soup to cool completely, then transfer to a sealable freezerproof container, making sure the meat is covered by liquid (add a little more cold stock if it isn't). Freeze for up to 3 months. To serve, defrost overnight in the refrigerator, then reheat gently in a saucepan at a low simmer until piping hot. Add a little hot water if the soup is too thick. Alternatively, reheat in a microwave on Medium for 2–3 minutes, then stir and heat for a further 2–3 minutes until piping hot. Leave the soup to stand for 5 minutes. Stir in some parsley to serve.

GOOD WITH Fresh crusty bread.

serves 8

**prep 20 mins
• cook 2 hrs**

Split pea and bacon soup

This thick soup is a pleasure to eat. The bacon adds flavour, but can be left out for vegetarians.

INGREDIENTS

2 tbsp olive oil
425g (15oz) bacon or pancetta,
    chopped into bite-sized pieces
2 onions, finely chopped
salt and freshly ground black pepper
4 celery sticks, finely chopped
4 carrots, finely chopped
550g (1¼lb) yellow split peas
1.7 litres (3 pints) hot vegetable stock

METHOD

1 Heat half the oil in a large heavy-based pan, add the bacon or pancetta, and cook over a medium heat, stirring occasionally, for 5 minutes, or until crispy and golden. Remove with a slotted spoon and put to one side. Heat the remaining oil in the pan, add the onions, and cook over a low heat for 6–8 minutes, or until soft and translucent. Season with salt and pepper, then add the celery and carrots and cook on a low heat for 5 minutes.

2 Add the yellow split peas and stock and bring to the boil slowly. Cover with a lid, reduce to a simmer, and cook for 2 hours, or until the peas are tender. Check occasionally, and top up with hot water if the soup begins to look too thick. Transfer to a blender or food processor and whiz until smooth and blended. Return to the pan with the bacon or pancetta to heat through, then taste and season with salt and pepper if needed.

FREEZING INSTRUCTIONS Leave the soup to cool completely, then transfer to a sealable freezerproof container, making sure the bacon pieces are covered by liquid. Freeze for up to 3 months. To serve, defrost overnight in the refrigerator, then reheat gently in a saucepan until piping hot. Add a little hot water if the soup is too thick. Alternatively, reheat in a microwave on Medium for 2–3 minutes, then stir and heat for a further 2–3 minutes until piping hot. Leave to stand for 5 minutes before serving.

GOOD WITH Fresh crusty bread.

serves 8

prep 15 mins
• cook 2 hrs
20 mins

blender or
food processor

Black bean and coconut soup

Exotic flavours make this soup a great way to start a spicy main course.

INGREDIENTS
2 tbsp olive oil
2 red onions, finely chopped
2 bay leaves
salt and freshly ground black pepper
4 garlic cloves, grated or finely chopped
2 tsp ground cumin
2 tsp ground coriander
1 tsp chilli powder
2 x 400g cans black beans, drained and rinsed
1.2 litres (2 pints) hot vegetable stock
400ml can coconut milk

METHOD
1 Heat the oil in a large pan, add the onions and bay leaves, and cook over a low heat for 6–8 minutes, or until the onions are soft and translucent. Season well with salt and pepper. Stir through the garlic, cumin, coriander, and chilli powder and cook for a few seconds.

2 Stir through the black beans, then pour in the stock and coconut milk. Bring to the boil, then reduce to a simmer and cook for 15–20 minutes. Remove the bay leaves and discard, then transfer the rest of the soup to a blender or food processor and pulse a couple of times so some of the beans are puréed and some remain whole. Return to the pan and heat through, adding a little more hot stock if it is too thick. Taste and season again with salt and pepper if needed.

FREEZING INSTRUCTIONS Leave the soup to cool completely, then freeze in a sealable freezerproof container for up to 3 months. To serve, defrost in the refrigerator overnight, then reheat gently in a saucepan until piping hot. Alternatively, reheat in a microwave on Medium for 2–3 minutes, then stir and heat for a further 2–3 minutes until piping hot. Leave the soup to stand for 5 minutes before serving.

GOOD WITH Tortilla triangles.

serves 8

prep 15 mins
• cook 30 mins

blender or
food processor

Chunky minestrone soup

Italians make this big, generous soup with seasonal vegetables. The staple ingredients, however, are hearty beans, tomatoes, and pasta.

INGREDIENTS

2 tbsp olive oil
2 onions, finely chopped
3 garlic cloves, grated or finely chopped
4 celery sticks, finely chopped
4 carrots, finely chopped
250g (9oz) pancetta, cut into small cubes
handful of flat-leaf parsley, finely chopped
handful of sage leaves, finely chopped
2 tbsp tomato purée
2 x 400g cans chopped tomatoes

2 x 400g cans borlotti beans, drained and rinsed
salt and freshly ground black pepper
2.3 litres (4 pints) hot chicken stock
225g (8oz) fresh or frozen peas
300g (10oz) runner beans, trimmed
   and cut into 3
300g (10oz) small pasta shapes
   such as ditalini (or spaghetti,
   cut into 1cm (^{1}/$_2$in) pieces)
freshly grated Parmesan cheese, to serve

METHOD

1 Heat the oil in a large pan, add the onions, and cook over a low heat for 6–8 minutes, or until soft and translucent. Add the garlic, celery, and carrots, and cook over a low heat, stirring occasionally, for 10 minutes, or until soft. Stir in the pancetta and cook for 5 minutes, or until golden.

2 Add the herbs, tomato purée, tomatoes, and beans and stir to combine. Season with salt and pepper, then pour in the stock. Bring to the boil, cover with a lid, and simmer for 40 minutes. Add the peas and beans for the last 5 minutes of cooking. Add the pasta, and simmer until piping hot and the pasta is cooked but still firm to the bite. Taste, and season again, if necessary. Top with Parmesan cheese, and serve.

FREEZING INSTRUCTIONS Leave to cool completely, then transfer to a sealable freezerproof container, making sure the pancetta and pasta are completely immersed in liquid. Freeze for up to 3 months. To serve, defrost in the refrigerator overnight, then reheat gently in a saucepan until piping hot. Serve with a sprinkle of grated Parmesan cheese.

GOOD WITH Fresh crusty bread.

serves 8

prep 25 mins
• cook 1 hr

healthy option

CASSEROLES & CURRIES

Peel and chop garlic

Garlic is essential to many recipes and preparing it is easy once you know how. The finer you chop garlic, the more flavour you'll release.

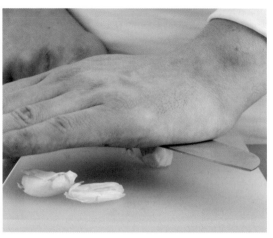

1 Lay each garlic clove flat on a cutting board. Place the side of a large knife on top of the clove and press firmly on the flat of the blade to break the garlic skin.

2 Cut the ends off the clove and discard the skin. Slice the garlic lengthways, then cut across into small chunks. Collect the pieces into a pile and chop again for finer pieces.

Chop onion

Once an onion is halved, it can be sliced or diced. This technique is for quick dicing, which helps prevent your eyes from watering.

1 Peel and cut the onion in half, then lay the cut side down. Slice down through the layers vertically, cutting up to, but not through, the root end.

2 Cut across the vertical slices to produce an even dice. Use the root to hold the onion steady, then discard when all the onion is diced.

Chop herbs

Chop fresh herbs just before using to release their flavour and aroma. You may wish to reserve a small amount to use as a garnish for the finished dish.

1 Strip the leaves from their stems and gather them together in a tight pile. If using large-leafed herbs, such as basil (shown), layer them and roll them up gently.

2 Using a large, sharp knife, slice through the herbs. Then gather into a pile and chop through the herbs using a rocking motion. To chop more finely, gather and repeat to achieve the desired size.

Deseed and cut chillies

Chillies contain capsaicin, which gives off a fiery heat. Always wash your hands immediately after handling chillies.

1 Cut the chilli lengthways in half. Using the tip of your knife, scrape out the seeds and remove the membrane and stem.

2 Flatten each half with the palm of your hand and slice lengthways into strips. To dice, hold the strips firmly together and slice crossways.

Mixed bean medley

Wholesome and tasty, this one-pot meal makes a good supper dish.

INGREDIENTS

1 tbsp olive oil
1 onion, finely chopped
salt
2 garlic cloves, grated or finely chopped
100g (3½oz) bacon lardons or pancetta cubes
pinch of chilli flakes
2 tsp dried oregano
400g can mixed beans, drained and rinsed
300ml (10fl oz) pale ale
900ml (1½ pints) hot vegetable stock

METHOD

1 Heat the oil in a large, heavy, deep-sided frying pan over a low heat. Add the onion and a pinch of salt, and sweat gently for about 5 minutes. Stir through the garlic, and cook for about 30 seconds more without colouring.

2 Increase the heat slightly, and add the bacon or pancetta. Cook for about 5 minutes until it begins to turn golden. Sprinkle over the chilli flakes and oregano, and tip in the beans. Stir through.

3 Pour in the ale, bring to the boil, and cook over a high heat for a good 5 minutes. Add the stock, reduce the heat slightly, and simmer gently for 20–25 minutes, stirring occasionally, until the mixture thickens. Serve hot.

FREEZING INSTRUCTIONS Leave to cool completely, then freeze in a sealable freezerproof container for up to 3 months. To serve, defrost in the refrigerator overnight, then reheat gently in a saucepan, topping up with water as needed, until piping hot. Alternatively, reheat in a microwave on Medium for 2–3 minutes, then stir and heat for a further 2–3 minutes until piping hot. Leave to stand for 5 minutes before serving.

GOOD WITH Fresh crusty bread to mop up the flavoursome gravy.

serves 4

prep 10 mins
• cook 40 mins

healthy option

Couscous royale

This richly spiced dish makes a colourful Moroccan feast.

INGREDIENTS

2 tbsp olive oil
600g (1lb 5oz) lean lamb leg, cut into chunks
6 chicken drumsticks and thighs
1 large red onion, sliced
2 garlic cloves, grated or finely chopped
1 red pepper, deseeded and diced
1 aubergine, diced
4 tsp harissa paste
1 tbsp paprika
1 tsp ground turmeric
2 courgettes, sliced

200ml (7fl oz) chicken stock
400g can chickpeas, drained
400g can chopped tomatoes
175g (6oz) chorizo or cooked Merguez
    sausage, thickly sliced
salt and freshly ground black pepper
large sprig of thyme
1 bay leaf
450g (1lb) couscous, cooked according
    to packet instructions
chopped coriander leaves, to garnish

METHOD

1 Heat the oil in the casserole and brown the lamb and chicken in batches, turning occasionally. Remove from the pan and set aside to drain on kitchen paper.

2 Add the onion, garlic, pepper, and aubergine and fry, stirring, for 3–4 minutes. Stir in the harissa, paprika, and turmeric, and cook for a further 1 minute.

3 Return the lamb and chicken to the casserole, add the courgettes, chicken stock, chickpeas, tomatoes, and chorizo, and season to taste with salt and pepper. Bring to the boil, then add the thyme and bay leaf, reduce the heat, cover tightly, and simmer gently over a low heat for 1 hour, or until the meats are tender.

4 Strain off the liquid, pour it into a wide pan, and bring to the boil, until slightly reduced.

5 Stir the meats and vegetables into the cooked couscous. Pour the reserved liquid over, and sprinkle with chopped coriander to serve.

FREEZING INSTRUCTIONS Omit the couscous if freezing. Prepare the recipe to the end of step 3, then leave to cool. Transfer to a sealable freezerproof container, making sure the meat is completely covered with the sauce (top up with stock if needed), and freeze for up to 2 months. To thaw, defrost overnight in the refrigerator. To serve, prepare the couscous according to packet instructions and set to one side. Reheat the meat mixture in a saucepan, topping up with water as needed to prevent scorching, until piping hot. Stir through the couscous and serve sprinkled with some chopped coriander.

serves 6

**prep 10 mins
• cook 1 hr
20 mins**

**large
flameproof
casserole**

Vegetable curry

Indians consider cardamom, cloves, coriander, and cumin seeds to be "warming spices" that heat the body from within, making this an excellent winter dish.

INGREDIENTS

4 tbsp ghee or sunflower oil
300g (10oz) waxy potatoes, diced
5 green cardamom pods, cracked
3 cloves
1 cinnamon stick, broken in half
2 tsp cumin seeds
1 onion, finely chopped
2 tsp peeled and grated fresh root ginger
2 large garlic cloves, crushed
1½ tsp turmeric
1 tsp ground coriander

salt and freshly ground black pepper
400g can chopped tomatoes
pinch of sugar
2 carrots, peeled and diced
2 green chillies, deseeded (optional) and sliced
150g (5½oz) Savoy cabbage or green cabbage, sliced
150g (5½oz) cauliflower florets
150g (5½oz) peas
2 tbsp chopped coriander leaves
almond flakes, toasted, to garnish

METHOD

1 Melt the ghee or heat the oil in a large deep-sided frying pan over a high heat. Add the potatoes and stir fry for 5 minutes, or until golden brown. Remove from the pan with a slotted spoon and set aside to drain on kitchen paper.

2 Reduce the heat to medium, add the cardamom pods, cloves, cinnamon, and cumin seeds, stirring just until the seeds begin to crackle. Add the onion and continue stir-frying for 5–8 minutes, or until softened. Add the ginger, garlic, turmeric, and ground coriander, then season to taste with salt and pepper and stir for 1 minute.

3 Stir in the tomatoes and sugar. Return the potatoes to the pan, add the carrots, chillies, and 250ml (9fl oz) water, and bring to the boil, stirring often. Reduce the heat to low and simmer for 15 minutes, or until the carrots are just tender, stirring occasionally. Add a little water, if needed.

4 Stir in the cabbage, cauliflower, and peas, and increase the heat to medium. Let the liquid gently bubble for a further 5–10 minutes, or until all the vegetables are tender. Stir in the coriander leaves and adjust the seasoning, if necessary. Remove and discard the cardamom pods, cloves, and cinnamon stick. Transfer to a serving bowl and sprinkle with almond flakes.

FREEZING INSTRUCTIONS Leave to cool completely, then transfer to a sealable freezerproof container, making sure the vegetables are covered with sauce. Freeze for up to 3 months. To serve, defrost in the refrigerator overnight, then reheat in a saucepan, topping up with water if needed, until piping hot. Alternatively, reheat in a microwave at Medium for 2–3 minutes, then stir and heat for a further 2–3 minutes until piping hot.

GOOD WITH Freshly boiled basmati rice, or naan bread.

serves 4–6

prep 20 mins
• cook
35–45 mins

Chunky ratatouille

This French classic is full of tasty vegetables and is an excellent healthy choice.

INGREDIENTS

1 tbsp olive oil
1 onion, finely chopped
salt and freshly ground black pepper
1 bay leaf
2 garlic cloves, thinly sliced
1–2 tsp dried oregano
pinch of fennel seeds
1 aubergine, cut into chunky pieces
1 small glass of red wine
150ml (5fl oz) tomato juice
2 small courgettes, cut into chunky pieces
3 tomatoes, roughly chopped
large handful of Swiss chard leaves
flat-leaf parsley, freshly chopped, to garnish

METHOD

1 Heat the oil in a large pan over a low heat. Add the onion, a pinch of salt, and the bay leaf, and sweat for 5 minutes until the onion is soft and translucent.

2 Add the garlic, oregano, fennel seeds, aubergine, and wine. Let simmer for a minute, then add the tomato juice. Cook for about 10 minutes until the aubergine is soft.

3 Now add the courgettes and tomatoes, and cook for a further 5–10 minutes. Stir through the Swiss chard, and cook for another couple of minutes until all the vegetables are tender. Taste, and season if needed.

4 Garnish with the chopped parsley, and serve hot.

FREEZING INSTRUCTIONS Leave to cool completely, then transfer to a sealable freezerproof container, making sure the Swiss chard is immersed in liquid. Freeze for up to 3 months. To serve, defrost in the refrigerator overnight, then reheat gently in a saucepan, topping up with hot stock if needed, until piping hot. Garnish with chopped parsley to serve.

GOOD WITH Fluffy rice or some fresh crusty bread.

serves 4

prep 15 mins
• cook 30 mins

healthy option

Pearl barley and borlotti bean one-pot

Hearty beans and barley simmered in wine make this a warming, comforting dish for a winter day.

INGREDIENTS

1 tbsp olive oil
1 onion, finely chopped
1 small glass of red wine
175g (6oz) pearl barley
400g can borlotti beans, drained and rinsed
400g can chopped plum tomatoes
1.2 litres (2 pints) hot vegetable stock
salt and freshly ground black pepper
chilli oil, to serve (optional)

METHOD

1 Heat the oil in a large heavy pan over a low heat. Add the onion and a pinch of salt, and sweat gently for 5 minutes until soft and translucent. Increase the heat, pour in the wine, and simmer for about 5 minutes.

2 Reduce the heat to low, add the pearl barley, and stir well until it has soaked up all the liquid. Tip in the borlotti beans, tomatoes, and hot stock. Bring to the boil again, and keep boiling for a further 5 minutes.

3 Reduce the heat to low once again, season well with salt and pepper, and gently simmer for 25–40 minutes until the pearl barley is cooked and all the stock has been absorbed. If the mixture starts to dry out, add a little hot water.

4 Drizzle over a splash of chilli oil (if using), and serve hot.

FREEZING INSTRUCTIONS Leave to cool, then freeze in a sealable freezerproof container for up to 3 months. To serve, defrost in the refrigerator overnight, then reheat in a saucepan, topping up with hot water if needed. Simmer gently for 15–20 minutes, or until piping hot. Alternatively, reheat in a microwave, topping up with water if the consistency is too thick, on Medium for 2–3 minutes, then stir and heat for a further 2–3 minutes until piping hot. Leave to stand for 5 minutes. Serve with a drizzle of chilli oil, if using.

GOOD WITH Fresh crusty bread.

serves 4

prep 10 mins
• cook 1 hr

healthy option

CASSEROLES & CURRIES

Chickpea curry with cardamom

Fragrant spices and chickpeas combine in this home-style Indian curry.

INGREDIENTS

1 tbsp vegetable oil
1 onion, finely chopped
salt and freshly ground black pepper
1 tsp cumin seeds
1 tsp ground turmeric
1 tsp ground coriander
6 green cardamom pods, lightly crushed
400g can chickpeas, drained and rinsed
400g can whole peeled plum tomatoes,
   chopped in the can
1–2 tsp garam masala
1 tsp chilli powder (more if you like it hot)

METHOD

1 Heat the oil in a large heavy pan over a low heat. Add the onion and a pinch of salt, and sweat gently for about 5 minutes until soft and translucent. Stir in the cumin seeds, turmeric, coriander, and cardamom, and continue cooking for about 5 minutes until fragrant.

2 Add the chickpeas to the pan, and stir through well, crushing them slightly with the back of a wooden spoon. Tip in the tomatoes, including any juices, then fill the can with water and add this also. Sprinkle in the garam masala and chilli powder, raise the heat and bring to the boil.

3 Reduce the heat to low, and simmer gently for about 20 minutes, until the sauce begins to thicken slightly. Season with salt and pepper.

FREEZING INSTRUCTIONS Leave to cool completely, then transfer to a sealable freezerproof container and freeze for up to 3 months. To serve, defrost in the refrigerator overnight, then reheat in a saucepan, topping up with hot water if needed. Simmer gently until piping hot. Alternatively, reheat in a microwave, topping up with hot water if needed, on Medium for 2–3 minutes, then stir and heat for a further 2–3 minutes until piping hot.

GOOD WITH Naan bread or basmati rice.

serves 4

prep 10 mins
• cook 30 mins

healthy option

58

Braised turkey with vegetables

Fresh flavours of lemon and tarragon enliven this recipe.

INGREDIENTS

2 tbsp olive oil
knob of butter
4 turkey breast fillets
salt and freshly ground black pepper
2 onions, sliced
2 carrots, sliced
1 fennel bulb, sliced
a few tarragon leaves, roughly chopped
600ml (1 pint) hot chicken stock
handful of flat-leaf parsley, finely chopped, to serve
grated zest of 1 lemon, to serve

METHOD

1 Preheat the oven to 180°C (350°F/Gas 4). Heat the oil and butter gently in a large frying pan. Season the turkey well with salt and pepper, then cook over a medium heat, stirring occasionally, for 10 minutes, or until lightly golden all over. Transfer to a shallow casserole dish.

2 Add the vegetables and tarragon and season well with salt and pepper. Pour in enough stock so that it comes almost to the top of the dish, but doesn't cover the ingredients. Cover with a lid and cook in the oven for 40 minutes, or until the turkey and vegetables are tender. Top with the parsley and lemon zest, and serve hot with a pinch of pepper.

FREEZING INSTRUCTIONS Leave to cool completely, then remove the turkey and slice the meat. Transfer to a sealable freezerproof container, making sure the turkey is well covered with the sauce (add a little more cold stock if it isn't). Freeze for up to 3 months. To serve, defrost in the refrigerator overnight, then reheat in a saucepan, topping up with hot water if needed. Simmer gently for 15–20 minutes, or until piping hot. Alternatively, reheat in a microwave on High for 3–4 minutes, then stir and heat for a further 3–4 minutes until piping hot. Leave to stand for 5 minutes. Serve with chopped parsley and lemon zest.

GOOD WITH Crushed boiled new potatoes.

serves 8

prep 20 mins
• cook 40 mins

healthy option

Coq au vin

This quick version of the famous dish from Burgundy is brilliant for a family Sunday lunch.

INGREDIENTS
50g (1³/₄oz) butter
3 tbsp olive oil
2 large onions, diced
10 garlic cloves, chopped
300g (10oz) unsmoked streaky bacon, chopped
2 tbsp thyme leaves
750g (1lb 10oz) button mushrooms
salt and freshly ground black pepper
1 litre (1³/₄ pints) good red wine
1 litre (1³/₄ pints) hot chicken stock
1.1kg (2¹/₂lb) chicken pieces, skinned

METHOD
1 Heat the butter and oil in a large heavy-based pan over a medium heat, add the onions, and cook for 5 minutes, or until starting to soften. Add the garlic and bacon and cook for 5 minutes, stirring frequently. Add the thyme and mushrooms, season with salt and pepper, and cook for 2 minutes.

2 Pour in the wine, raise the heat, and allow to boil for 5 minutes while the alcohol evaporates. Pour in the stock, bring to the boil, then add the chicken pieces. Combine well, bring to the boil again, then lower the heat and simmer for 25 minutes. Serve hot.

FREEZING INSTRUCTIONS Leave to cool, then transfer to a sealable freezerproof container, making sure the chicken is completely covered by the sauce. Freeze for up to 3 months. To serve, defrost overnight in the refrigerator, then transfer to a casserole dish, cover, and reheat in an oven preheated to 180°C (350°F/Gas 4) for 25 minutes, or until piping hot. Add a little hot water or hot stock if the casserole starts to dry out.

GOOD WITH Parsley buttered potatoes or fresh crusty French bread.

serves 8

prep 15 mins
• cook 40 mins

Caribbean stew with allspice and ginger

Scotch bonnet chillies are very fiery so adjust the amount you use according to how hot you want your stew to be.

INGREDIENTS

1–2 Scotch Bonnet chillies
  (according to taste), deseeded
2 tsp allspice
handful of thyme leaves
2 tsp tamarind paste
5cm (2in) piece fresh root ginger,
  peeled and roughly chopped
salt and freshly ground black pepper

3 tbsp olive oil
4 large chicken breast fillets, skinned
  and cut into bite-sized pieces
1 tbsp plain flour
1.4 litres (2½ pints) hot chicken stock
4 mixed peppers, deseeded and roughly
  chopped
5 tomatoes, skinned and roughly chopped

METHOD

1 Put the chillies, allspice, thyme, tamarind, ginger, and some salt and pepper in a blender or food processor and whiz to a paste. Add a little of the oil and whiz again. Pour the paste into a plastic bag, add the chicken, and squish together. Leave to marinate for 30 minutes, or overnight in the refrigerator.

2 Heat the remaining oil in a large cast-iron pan or flameproof casserole, add the chicken and marinade, and cook, stirring often, over medium heat for 10 minutes, or until the chicken is golden. Stir in the flour, then add a little of the stock, and stir to scrape up any crispy bits from the bottom of the pan. Pour in the rest of the stock and keep stirring until the flour has blended in.

3 Stir in the peppers and tomatoes and season well with salt and pepper. Bring to the boil, then reduce to a simmer and cook over a low heat for 30 minutes, or until the sauce has begun to thicken slightly. Taste, and season again if needed.

FREEZING INSTRUCTIONS Leave to cool completely, then transfer to a sealable freezerproof container, making sure the chicken is well covered with sauce. Freeze for up to 3 months. To serve, defrost in the refrigerator overnight, then transfer to casserole dish, cover, and reheat in an oven preheated to 180°C (350°F/Gas 4) for 30–40 minutes, or until piping hot. Add a little hot water or hot stock if the stew starts to dry out.

GOOD WITH Baked sweet potatoes or sweet potato mash.

serves 8

**prep 30 mins,
plus marinating
• cook 30 mins**

**blender or food
processor
• large cast-iron
pan or
flameproof
casserole**

Chicken korma

A creamy, aromatic, mild curry popular in Indian restaurants.

INGREDIENTS
4 tbsp vegetable oil or ghee
8 skinless boneless chicken thighs,
    cut into 2.5cm (1in) pieces
2 large onions, thinly sliced
1 tbsp ground coriander
1 tbsp ground cumin
1 tsp ground turmeric
$^{1}/_{2}$ tsp ground ginger
1 tsp chilli powder
1 tsp ground cardamom
2 garlic cloves, crushed
150g (5$^{1}/_{2}$oz) thick plain yogurt
1 tbsp plain flour
300ml (10fl oz) chicken stock
150ml (5fl oz) double cream
1 tbsp lemon juice

METHOD
1 Heat half of the oil in a large pan and fry the chicken in batches over a high heat until lightly browned on both sides. Remove from the pan and set aside.

2 Lower the heat, add the rest of the oil to the pan, and fry the onions until soft and golden. Add the spices and garlic and fry for 2 minutes, stirring occasionally. Gradually stir in the yogurt.

3 Put the flour in a small bowl, add a little stock and mix to a smooth paste. Pour the paste into the pan with the rest of the stock and bring to the boil, stirring constantly, then lower the heat. Return the chicken to the pan and simmer gently, for 15 minutes, or until cooked through, stirring occasionally.

4 Stir in the cream and lemon juice and simmer for a further 5 minutes before serving.

FREEZING INSTRUCTIONS Leave to cool completely, then transfer to a sealable freezerproof container, making sure the chicken is well covered with sauce. Freeze for up to 1 month. To serve, defrost in the refrigerator overnight, then reheat gently in a pan until piping hot.

GOOD WITH Herb-flecked boiled rice, naan bread, and a variety of chutneys.

serves 4

prep 20 mins
• cook 45 mins

Baked chicken with onion, garlic, and tomatoes

Simple ingredients are slow-cooked to make this a dish to savour.

INGREDIENTS

8 chicken pieces, skin on
salt and freshly ground black pepper
1 tbsp plain flour
2 tbsp olive oil
6 streaky bacon rashers, chopped
1 onion, finely chopped
2 garlic cloves, grated or finely chopped
3 celery sticks, finely chopped
3 carrots, finely chopped
1 small glass of dry white wine
400g can peeled whole plum tomatoes, chopped
300ml (10fl oz) hot vegetable stock

METHOD

1 Preheat the oven to 200°C (400°F/Gas 6). Season the chicken well with salt and pepper, then dust with the flour.

2 Heat 1 tbsp of the oil in a large flameproof casserole (preferably a cast-iron one) over a high heat. Add the chicken pieces, skin-side down, together with the bacon, and cook the chicken for 5–8 minutes on each side until everything is golden. Remove from the pan, and set aside.

3 Reduce the heat to low, and add the remaining oil to the casserole with the onion and a pinch of salt. Sweat for about 5 minutes until soft, then add the garlic, celery, and carrots. Sweat for a further 5–6 minutes until soft.

4 Increase the heat to high once again, and add the wine. Let boil for a few minutes until the alcohol has evaporated. Tip in the tomatoes and their juices, and pour in the stock. Gently boil for a few minutes more. Reduce the heat to a simmer, and return the chicken and bacon to the casserole. Stir through, cover, and transfer to the oven to cook for about 1 hour. Top up with more stock or hot water if it begins to dry out.

FREEZING INSTRUCTIONS Leave to cool, then transfer to a sealable freezerproof container, making sure the chicken is completely covered by the sauce. Freeze for up to 3 months. To serve, defrost overnight in the refrigerator, then transfer to a casserole dish, cover, and reheat in an oven preheated to 180°C (350°F/Gas 4) for 30–40 minutes, or until piping hot. Add a little hot water or hot stock if the casserole starts to dry out.

GOOD WITH Creamy mashed potato.

serves 4

prep 5 mins
• cook 1 hr
30 mins

flameproof
casserole

Chicken and cornmeal cobbler

This dish uses minimal fat so is a good healthy option.

INGREDIENTS

2 tbsp olive oil

6 skinless boneless chicken breasts,
  cut into bite-sized pieces

salt and freshly ground black pepper

2 red onions, finely sliced

4 celery stalks, roughly chopped

2 glasses of red wine

5 carrots, roughly chopped

900ml (1½ pints) hot vegetable stock

150g (5½oz) plain flour,
  plus a little extra to dust

150g (5½oz) cornmeal

50g (1¾oz) butter

handful of flat-leaf parsley, finely chopped

splash of milk

1 egg yolk, lightly beaten

METHOD

1 Heat half the oil in a large shallow cast-iron pan or flameproof casserole, season the chicken with salt and pepper, then cook over medium heat, turning occasionally, for 10 minutes, or until lightly golden all over. Remove with a slotted spoon and put to one side.

2 Preheat the oven to 180°C (350°F/Gas 4). Heat the remaining oil in the pan, then add the onions and cook over low heat for 6–8 minutes, or until soft. Add the celery and cook for 5 minutes, or until soft. Pour in the wine, raise the heat, and allow to boil for a couple of minutes while the alcohol evaporates. Add the carrots, return the chicken to the pan, then season well with salt and pepper. Pour in the stock and cook, uncovered, over a low heat, stirring occasionally, for 1 hour, or until all the ingredients are tender. Top up with a little hot water if it begins to look dry.

3 Meanwhile, put the flour, cornmeal, and a pinch of salt in a large mixing bowl. Add the butter and rub it in with your fingertips until you have a breadcrumb texture. Stir through parsley, then add the milk a little at a time until the dough comes together. Form into a ball and put in the refrigerator to rest for 20 minutes. Flatten the chilled dough out on a floured surface, then roll it out with a rolling pin. Cut out about 18 rounds using the cutter, then add to the casserole, brushing them with egg yolk, before you put the pan into the oven for 30 minutes to cook the cobbler rounds.

FREEZING INSTRUCTIONS Leave to cool completely, then transfer to a sealable freezerproof container, making sure the meat is completely covered by sauce. Freeze for up to 3 months. To serve, defrost overnight in the refrigerator, then transfer to a casserole dish, loosely cover with foil, and reheat in an oven preheated to 180°C (350°F/Gas 4). Cook for 30–40 minutes until piping hot, adding a little hot stock if it starts to dry out. Remove the foil for the last 10 minutes of reheating.

serves 8

prep 20 mins
• cook 1 hr
45 mins

healthy option

large
flameproof
casserole
• 4cm (1½in)
cutter

Chicken jalfrezi

A spicy dish with chillies and mustard seeds, for those who like their curries hot.

INGREDIENTS

2 tbsp sunflower oil
2 tsp ground cumin
2 tsp yellow mustard seeds
1 tsp ground turmeric
2 tbsp masala curry paste
2.5cm (1in) piece fresh root ginger, peeled and finely chopped
3 garlic cloves, crushed
1 onion, sliced
1 red pepper, deseeded and sliced
$^1/_2$ green pepper, deseeded and sliced
2 green chillies, deseeded and finely chopped
675g (1$^1/_2$lb) skinless boneless chicken thighs or breasts,
   cut into 2.5cm (1in) pieces
225g can chopped tomatoes
3 tbsp chopped coriander leaves
salt

METHOD

1 Heat the oil in a large pan over a medium heat, add the cumin, mustard seeds, turmeric, and curry paste, and stir-fry for 1–2 minutes.

2 Add the ginger, garlic, and onion and fry, stirring frequently, until the onion starts to soften. Add the red and green peppers and the chillies and fry for 5 minutes.

3 Increase the heat to medium-high, add the chicken, and fry until starting to brown. Add the tomatoes and coriander, reduce the heat, and simmer for 10 minutes, or until the chicken is cooked through, stirring often. Taste and season with salt, if needed. Serve hot.

FREEZING INSTRUCTIONS Leave to cool completely, then transfer to a sealable freezerproof container, making sure the chicken is covered by sauce. Freeze for up to 3 months. To serve, defrost overnight in the refrigerator, then reheat gently in a pan, adding a little water if needed. Simmer for 15–20 minutes until piping hot. Alternatively, reheat in a microwave at High for 2–4 minutes, stir, and heat for a further 2–4 minutes until piping hot. Leave to stand for 5 minutes before serving.

GOOD WITH Basmati rice and poppadums.

serves 4

**prep 20 mins
• cook 25 mins**

healthy option

Garlic and chilli chicken with honey sweet potato

A sweet, comforting dish that has a piquant character from the chillies.

INGREDIENTS

8 chicken pieces (a mixture of thighs and drumsticks), skin on
salt and freshly ground black pepper
4 sweet potatoes, peeled and roughly chopped
1–2 tbsp clear honey
2 tbsp olive oil
2 red chillies, deseeded and sliced
a few sprigs of thyme
$1/2$ garlic bulb, cloves separated, peeled, and squashed
1 small glass of dry white wine
300ml (10fl oz) hot light chicken stock

METHOD

1 Preheat the oven to 200°C (400°F/Gas 6). Season the chicken liberally with salt and pepper, and coat the sweet potatoes in the honey.

2 In a heavy flameproof casserole, preferably a cast-iron one, heat 1 tbsp of the oil over a medium heat. Add the sweet potatoes, and cook for about 5 minutes until beginning to colour, then remove from the pan and set aside.

3 Increase the heat to medium-high, and heat the remaining oil in the same pan. Brown the chicken for about 5 minutes on each side until nicely golden all over. Add the chillies, thyme, and garlic. Return the sweet potatoes to the pan, and season well.

4 Pour in the wine and stock, cover the pan, and transfer to the oven to cook for 1 hour. Check the casserole a few times during cooking; give it a stir if needed, or add a small amount of stock if it is too dry.

FREEZING INSTRUCTIONS Leave to cool, then transfer to sealable freezerproof containers, making sure the chicken is completely covered by the sauce (add a little more cold stock if it isn't). Freeze for up to 3 months. To serve, defrost overnight in the refrigerator, then transfer to a casserole dish, and top up with a little hot stock. Cover, and reheat in an oven preheated to 180°C (350°F/Gas 4) for 30–40 minutes until piping hot. Add more hot stock if it starts to dry out.

GOOD WITH Chunks of fresh crusty bread.

serves 4

prep 15 mins
• cook 1 hr
10 mins

healthy option

flameproof
casserole

Shin of beef with Marsala

Marsala is a fortified wine from Sicily that is popular in Italian cooking. Puy lentils add extra body and flavour to this hearty casserole.

INGREDIENTS
1.6kg (3½lb) shin beef, cut into bite-sized pieces
plain flour, to dust
salt and freshly ground black pepper
3 tbsp olive oil
2 red onions, roughly chopped
4 carrots, roughly chopped
300ml (10fl oz) Marsala
200g (7oz) Puy lentils, rinsed and picked over
1.4 litres (2½ pints) hot vegetable stock
2 bay leaves

METHOD
1 Preheat the oven to 180°C (350°F/Gas 4). Dust the meat with a little flour, then season with salt and pepper. Heat half the oil in a flameproof casserole, add the meat, and cook over a medium heat, stirring often, for 10 minutes, or until brown on all sides. Remove with a slotted spoon and put to one side.

2 Heat the remaining oil in the pan, add the onions, and cook over a low heat for 6–8 minutes, or until soft and translucent. Stir in the carrots and cook for 5 minutes. Return the meat to the pan, pour in the Marsala, and let it boil for a few minutes while the alcohol evaporates. Stir in the lentils, add the stock, and bring to the boil. Season with salt and black pepper, then add the bay leaves. Cover with a lid and put in the oven to cook for 1½ hours. Check occasionally, and add a little hot water if it looks dry.

FREEZING INSTRUCTIONS Leave to cool completely, then transfer to a sealable freezerproof container, making sure the meat is well covered by sauce. Freeze for up to 3 months. To serve, defrost overnight in the refrigerator, then reheat gently in a pan, adding a little hot water if the sauce is too thick. Simmer for 15–20 minutes, or until piping hot. Alternatively, reheat in a microwave on High for 3–4 minutes, stir, and heat for a further 3–4 minutes until piping hot. Leave to stand for 5 minutes before serving.

GOOD WITH Fresh crusty bread.

serves 8

prep 25 mins
• cook 1 hr
30 mins

large
flameproof
casserole

Pork with fennel and mustard

If speed is what you need, this lively dish is an excellent quick fix.

INGREDIENTS

6 tbsp olive oil
2 large onions, sliced
3 fennel bulbs, sliced
1.1kg (2½lb) lean pork, cut into bite-sized pieces
8 garlic cloves, grated or finely chopped
150ml (5fl oz) dry white wine
2 tbsp wholegrain mustard
1 tsp paprika
large handful of flat-leaf parsley, chopped
1 tbsp sage leaves, chopped
1 tbsp rosemary leaves, chopped
2 tbsp plain flour
900ml (1½ pints) milk
salt and freshly ground black pepper

METHOD

1 Heat the oil in a large heavy-based pan, add the onions and fennel, and cook for 5 minutes, or until beginning to soften. Add the pork and cook, stirring occasionally, for 5 minutes, or until no longer pink. Add the garlic and cook for 1 minute, then stir in the wine and mustard, raise the heat, and allow to boil for 3 minutes while the alcohol evaporates.

2 Stir in the paprika, parsley, sage, and rosemary, then add the flour and mix well. Add a little of the milk, mix to a smooth paste, then stir in the rest of it. Season well with salt and pepper, and cook for 5 minutes, adding a little more milk if it looks dry.

FREEZING INSTRUCTIONS Leave to cool, then transfer to a sealable freezerproof container, making sure the pork is completely covered by the sauce. Freeze for up to 3 months. To serve, defrost overnight in the refrigerator, then transfer to a casserole dish, top up with a little hot stock, and cover. Reheat in an oven preheated to 180°C (350°F/Gas 4) for 25 minutes, or until piping hot. Add a little more stock if it starts to dry out.

GOOD WITH Crushed new potatoes or creamy mashed potatoes.

serves 8

prep 20 mins
• cook 20 mins

Pork goulash

This thick stew from Hungary is distinctive for its flavours of paprika, caraway seeds, garlic, and onion. It can also be made with beef.

INGREDIENTS

1.1kg (2½lb) stewing pork, cut into bite-sized pieces
1 tbsp plain flour
2 tsp paprika
2 tsp caraway seeds, crushed
salt and freshly ground black pepper
2 tbsp olive oil
1 tbsp cider vinegar
2 tbsp tomato purée
1.2 litres (2 pints) hot vegetable stock
6 tomatoes, skinned and roughly chopped
1 onion, sliced into rings, to serve
handful of curly parsley, finely chopped, to serve

METHOD

1 Toss the meat with the flour, paprika, and caraway seeds, and season well with salt and pepper. Heat the oil in a large cast-iron pan, then add the meat and cook over a high heat, stirring occasionally, for 8–10 minutes, or until it begins to brown. Add the vinegar and stir well for a couple of minutes, scraping up all the sticky bits from the bottom of the pan.

2 Add the tomato purée, followed by the stock, and bring to the boil. Reduce to a simmer, put a lid on, and cook gently for 1 hour. Check occasionally, and top up with boiling water if the goulash begins to dry out too much – it should be fairly thick, though.

3 Stir through the tomatoes, taste, and season again if needed, then top with the onion rings and parsley to serve.

FREEZING INSTRUCTIONS Leave to cool, then transfer to a sealable freezerproof container, making sure the pork and tomatoes are completely covered by the sauce. Freeze for up to 3 months. To serve, defrost overnight in the refrigerator, then reheat in a pan, topping up with a little hot water or hot stock. Simmer for 15–20 minutes, or until piping hot. Top with some onion rings and chopped parsley to serve.

GOOD WITH Steamed rice.

serves 8

prep 25 mins
• cook 1 hr

large
cast-iron pan

Lamb daube

One of the great Provençal dishes, daubes feature marinated meat that is braised slowly in wine. Orange zest, anise, and olives are typical ingredients.

INGREDIENTS

1.35kg (3lb) lamb (from the shoulder or leg), cut into bite-sized pieces
300ml (10fl oz) red wine
1 star anise
grated zest of 1 orange
salt and freshly ground black pepper
3 tbsp olive oil
2 onions, finely chopped

400g (14oz) bacon or pancetta, cut into bite-sized pieces
4 celery sticks, finely chopped
4 carrots, finely chopped
4 leeks, cleaned and cut into chunks
1.2 litres (2 pints) hot vegetable stock
2 handfuls of pitted green olives

METHOD

1 Put the lamb, wine, star anise, and orange zest in a bowl, season well with salt and pepper, and leave to marinate for 30 minutes, or overnight in the refrigerator.

2 Preheat the oven to 200°C (400°F/Gas 6). Heat half the oil in a flameproof casserole. Remove the meat with a slotted spoon (reserve the marinade) and add to the pan. Cook over a medium heat, stirring often, for 10 minutes or until browned all over. Remove with a slotted spoon and put to one side. Heat the remaining oil in the pan, add the onions, and cook over a low heat for 6–8 minutes, or until soft and translucent. Stir in the bacon or pancetta and cook for 6–10 minutes, or until crispy. Add the celery and carrots and cook over a low heat, adding more oil if needed, for 5 minutes, or until beginning to soften.

3 Stir in the leeks and cook for a couple of minutes, then return the meat to the pan and pour in the marinade and stock. Stir in the olives, bring to the boil, then season with salt and pepper. Cover with a lid and put in the oven to cook for 30 minutes. Turn the oven down to 150°C (300°F/Gas 2) and cook for a further 1^1/$_2$–2 hours. Check occasionally, and add a little hot water if it looks dry.

FREEZING INSTRUCTIONS Leave to cool completely, then transfer to a sealable freezerproof container, making sure the meat is well covered with the sauce. Freeze for up to 3 months. To serve, defrost overnight in the refrigerator, then reheat gently in a pan for 15–20 minutes until piping hot. Alternatively, place in a casserole dish, cover, and reheat in an oven preheated to 180°C (350°F/Gas 4) for 30–40 minutes, or until piping hot. Add a little hot stock if it starts to dry out.

GOOD WITH Sautéed potatoes.

serves 8

prep 25 mins, plus marinating • cook 2 hrs 30 mins

healthy option

large flameproof casserole

Pork with rice and tomatoes

Big, bold, and filling – this makes a super family meal.

INGREDIENTS

6 tbsp olive oil
3 onions, diced
1.1kg (2½lb) lean pork, cut into 5cm (2in) chunks
6 garlic cloves, grated or finely chopped
handful of flat-leaf parsley, chopped
1 tbsp thyme leaves, chopped
1 tbsp sage leaves, chopped
2 tsp paprika
150ml (5fl oz) dry white wine
550g (1¼lb) long-grain rice
4 x 400g cans chopped tomatoes
salt and freshly ground black pepper

METHOD

1 Preheat the oven to 150°C (300°F/Gas 2). Heat the oil in a large heavy-based pan, add the onions, and cook over a medium heat for 5 minutes, or until starting to soften. Add the pork and cook, stirring occasionally, for 5 minutes, or until no longer pink. Add the garlic, parsley, thyme, sage, and paprika and combine well, then add the wine and cook for 5 minutes. Add the rice and tomatoes, stir to combine, then season well with salt and pepper.

2 Cover with a lid and cook in the oven for 1 hour. Stir occasionally and add a little hot water if it starts to dry out. Remove from the oven and allow to stand for 10 minutes with the lid on before serving.

FREEZING INSTRUCTIONS Leave to cool completely, then transfer to sealable freezerproof containers, making sure the pork is well covered. Freeze for up to 1 month. To serve, defrost in the refrigerator overnight, then reheat in a microwave on High for 3–4 minutes, stir then heat for a further 3–4 minutes until piping hot. Leave to stand for 5 minutes before serving.

serves 6–8

prep 30 mins
• cook 1 hr

Sauerbraten

Wonderfully tender German-style beef with a richly spiced sauce.

INGREDIENTS

1kg (2¹/₄lb) boneless joint of beef,
   such as topside or rump
2 tbsp sunflower oil
1 onion, sliced
1 celery stick, chopped
1 tbsp plain flour
45g (1¹/₂oz) ginger nut biscuits, crushed
salt and freshly ground black pepper

For the marinade

400ml (14fl oz) red wine
150ml (5fl oz) red wine vinegar
2 onions, thinly sliced
1 tbsp light muscovado sugar
¹/₂ tsp freshly grated nutmeg
4 whole allspice berries, lightly crushed
4 black peppercorns, lightly crushed
2 bay leaves, crumbled
¹/₂ tsp salt

METHOD

1 To make the marinade, place the wine, vinegar, onions, sugar, nutmeg, allspice berries, peppercorns, bay leaves, salt, and 150ml (5fl oz) water in a pan. Stir over a high heat until boiling. Remove from the heat and leave to cool completely.

2 Place the meat in a bowl and pour in the cooled marinade. Cover with cling film and leave to marinate for 2–3 days in a refrigerator, turning the meat over twice each day.

3 Preheat the oven to 180°C (350°F/Gas 4). Lift the meat from the marinade, drain well, then pat dry with kitchen paper. Strain the marinade, discard the spices, and reserve the liquid.

4 Heat the oil in a large flameproof casserole and brown the meat on all sides. Remove the meat and set aside. Add the onion and celery to the pan and fry, stirring constantly, for 5–6 minutes, or until beginning to brown. Sprinkle the flour over the vegetables and stir over the heat for 1 minute, then stir in 400ml (14fl oz) of the reserved marinade. Stir until boiling.

5 Place the beef on top of the vegetables and baste with the liquid. Cover tightly and place in the oven for 2–2¹/₄ hours, or until the meat is tender when tested with a fork.

6 Lift the meat on to a warmed serving platter and cover loosely with foil. Strain the cooking liquid, pour it into a saucepan and boil rapidly to reduce to about 300ml (10fl oz). Add the ginger nut biscuits, stirring on the heat until the sauce is smooth. Season to taste with salt and pepper. Slice the meat and serve with the sauce.

FREEZING INSTRUCTIONS Leave to cool, then transfer to a sealable freezerproof container, making sure the meat is well covered with sauce. Freeze for up to 2 months. To serve, defrost in the refrigerator overnight, then cover with cling film and reheat in a microwave on High for 3–4 minutes. Stir, and heat for a further 3–4 minutes until piping hot.

GOOD WITH Whole roasted potatoes and carrots, or German potato dumplings and braised red cabbage.

serves 4–6

prep 30 mins,
plus marinating
• cook 2–2¹/₄ hrs

marinate for
2–3 days

large
flameproof
casserole

Beef and celeriac casserole with stout and anchovies

A rich casserole with earthy flavours.

INGREDIENTS

3 tbsp olive oil
1.1kg (2½lb) stewing steak or braising steak,
   cut into bite-sized pieces
2 onions, finely chopped
handful of thyme stalks
8 salted anchovies
1 large celeriac, peeled and cut into bite-sized pieces
500ml bottle stout
1.2 litres (2 pints) hot vegetable stock
salt and freshly ground black pepper
5 medium potatoes, cut into chunky pieces

METHOD

1 Preheat the oven to 180°C (350°F/Gas 4). Heat half the oil in a flameproof casserole, add the meat, and cook over a medium heat, stirring occasionally, for 10 minutes, or until browned all over. Remove with a slotted spoon and put to one side. Heat the remaining oil in the pan, add the onions and thyme, and cook over a low heat for 6–8 minutes, or until soft.

2 Stir in the anchovies, then stir in the celeriac and cook for 5–8 minutes. Add a little of the stout and stir to scrape up all the sticky bits from the bottom of the pan. Add the remaining stout and the stock, season with salt and pepper, then return the meat to the pan, cover with a lid, and put in the oven for 1 hour.

3 Add the potatoes, together with a little hot water if the casserole looks dry. Cook for a further 30 minutes.

FREEZING INSTRUCTIONS Leave to cool completely, then transfer to a sealable freezerproof container, making sure the meat is well covered with sauce. Freeze for up to 3 months. To serve, defrost in the refrigerator overnight, then reheat in a pan. Simmer gently for 15–20 minutes, topping up with hot water or hot stock if needed, or until piping hot. Alternatively, put in a casserole dish, cover, and reheat in an oven preheated to 180°C (350°F/Gas 4) for 30–40 minutes, or until piping hot.

GOOD WITH Colcannon or mashed potatoes and steamed cabbage.

serves 8

**prep 30 mins,
• cook 1 hr
30 mins**

**large
flameproof
casserole**

Pork and bean casserole

Using canned beans instead of dried ones makes this satisfying casserole quite quick to prepare.

INGREDIENTS

6 tbsp olive oil
3 large onions, diced
6 celery sticks, diced
1.1kg (2½lb) lean pork, cut into 2cm (¾in) dice
2 tsp paprika
400g can cannellini beans, drained and rinsed
400g can flageolet beans, drained and rinsed
400g can butter beans, drained and rinsed
8 garlic cloves, grated or finely chopped
150ml (5fl oz) dry white wine
300ml (10fl oz) hot vegetable stock
juice of 1 lemon
handful of flat-leaf parsley, chopped
salt and freshly ground black pepper

METHOD

1 Heat the oil in a large heavy-based pan over a medium heat, add the onions and celery, and cook, stirring frequently, for 5 minutes, or until soft. Add the pork and cook, stirring occasionally, for 5 minutes, or until no longer pink. Stir in the paprika, then add the beans and garlic and cook for 1 minute.

2 Stir in the wine and allow to boil for 3 minutes while the alcohol evaporates. Add the stock, lemon juice, and parsley, and season well with salt and pepper. Bring to the boil, then lower the heat and simmer for 20 minutes. Top up with hot water, if needed.

FREEZING INSTRUCTIONS Leave to cool, then transfer to a sealable freezerproof container, making sure the pork is completely covered by the sauce. Freeze for up to 3 months. To serve, defrost overnight in the refrigerator, then reheat gently in a pan for 15–20 minutes, or until piping hot. Add a little hot water or hot stock if it gets too dry. Alternatively, reheat in a microwave for 2–3 minutes on High, then stir and heat for a further 2–3 minutes, or until piping hot.

GOOD WITH Steamed rice.

serves 8

prep 20 mins
• cook 20 mins

healthy option

Lamb braised with green peas and preserved lemons

The fresh, herby flavours of this tagine-like dish are very appealing in summer.

INGREDIENTS

15g (½oz) flat-leaf parsley, chopped, plus extra to garnish
15g (½oz) coriander leaves, chopped, plus extra to garnish
1kg (2¼lb) leg of lamb, cut into slices
2 onions, finely chopped
3 garlic cloves, chopped
1 tsp peeled and grated fresh root ginger
9 tbsp olive oil
600ml (1 pint) meat stock
2 preserved lemons, cut into quarters, pulp removed
  and discarded, zest thinly sliced
450g (1lb) frozen peas
1 lemon, zest peeled into long, thin strips
  or cut into wedges, to garnish

METHOD

1 Combine the parsley, coriander, lamb, onions, garlic, ginger, and olive oil in a large dish and leave to marinate overnight, covered with cling film, in a refrigerator.

2 Remove the lamb with a slotted spoon and reserve the marinade. In a hot frying pan, brown the lamb evenly on all sides, then transfer to the casserole, pour over the reserved marinade, add the stock, and bring to the boil. Reduce the heat and simmer, covered, for 1 hour.

3 Add the preserved lemons to the pan, and continue simmering for another 30 minutes, or until the meat is very tender.

4 Adjust the seasoning if necessary, add the peas, and simmer for a further 5 minutes. Serve while still hot with chopped parsley and coriander sprinkled over, and garnish with lemon zest strips or with lemon wedges on the side.

FREEZING INSTRUCTIONS Leave to cool completely, then transfer to sealable freezerproof containers, making sure the lamb is completely covered by the sauce (add a little more cold stock if it isn't). Freeze for up to 3 months. To serve, defrost overnight in the refrigerator, then transfer to a casserole dish, and top up with a little hot stock. Cover, and reheat in an oven preheated to 180°C (350°F/Gas 4) for 30–40 minutes until piping hot. Add more hot stock if it starts to dry out. Serve with chopped parsley and coriander and lemon wedges.

GOOD WITH Couscous or rice.

serves 6

prep 15 mins,
plus marinating
• cook 1 hr
40 mins

marinate
overnight

large
flameproof
casserole

Chilli con carne

A really good chilli con carne recipe is a great staple for any kitchen.

INGREDIENTS

6 tbsp olive oil
3 large onions, diced
1.1kg (2^1/$_2$lb) lean minced beef
150ml (5fl oz) dry sherry
8 garlic cloves, chopped
4 green bird's-eye chillies, finely chopped
1 tsp cayenne pepper
1 tsp paprika
2 x 400g cans kidney beans, drained and rinsed
4 bay leaves
3 x 400g cans chopped tomatoes
2 tsp dried oregano
salt and freshly ground black pepper

METHOD

1 Heat the oil in a large heavy-based pan, add the onions, and cook, stirring frequently, for 5 minutes, or until starting to soften. Add the mince and cook, stirring constantly, for 5 minutes, or until no longer pink. Stir in the sherry and garlic and cook for 1 minute, then add the chillies, cayenne, and paprika, and cook for 5 minutes.

2 Add the kidney beans and bay leaves, cook for 2 minutes, then add the tomatoes and oregano. Bring to the boil, season well with salt and pepper, and simmer over a low heat for 40 minutes, stirring occasionally.

FREEZING INSTRUCTIONS Leave to cool, then transfer to sealable freezerproof containers. Freeze for up to 3 months. To serve, defrost overnight in the refrigerator, then reheat in a pan, topping up with a little water to prevent scorching. Simmer for 15–20 minutes, stirring frequently, until piping hot. Alternatively, reheat in a microwave on High for 2–3 minutes, then stir and heat for a further 2–3 minutes until piping hot. Leave to stand for 5 minutes before serving.

GOOD WITH Steamed or boiled rice.

serves 8

prep 30 mins
• cook 40 mins

healthy option

Spiced sausage cassoulet

A generous pinch of paprika lifts this classic French sausage-and-bean dish.

INGREDIENTS

4 tbsp olive oil
2 large onions, sliced
4 celery sticks, chopped
2 large potatoes, cut into 2cm (¾in) dice
24 pork chipolata sausages
200g (7oz) bacon lardons
6 garlic cloves, chopped
2 x 400g cans haricot beans,
    drained and rinsed
1 tbsp tomato purée

3 tsp paprika
2 tsp dried thyme
2 tsp dried oregano
1 tsp freshly ground black pepper
300ml (10fl oz) dry white wine
600ml (1 pint) hot vegetable stock
125g (4½oz) fresh breadcrumbs
handful of flat-leaf parsley, chopped
50g (1¾oz) butter

METHOD

1 Preheat the oven to 150°C (300°F/Gas 2). Heat the oil in a large heavy-based pan, add the onions, celery, and potatoes, and cook for 5 minutes, or until starting to soften. Add the sausages and lardons and cook for a further 5 minutes, or until starting to brown.

2 Add the garlic and cook for 1 minute, then add the haricot beans, tomato purée, paprika, thyme, oregano, and pepper. Combine well, then add the wine. Bring to the boil and simmer for 2 minutes, then add the stock and 300ml (10fl oz) of hot water. Bring to the boil, simmer for 10 minutes, then remove from the heat.

3 Mix the breadcrumbs with the parsley and cover the top of the dish with them. Dot with knobs of the butter, cover with a lid, and bake for 1½ hours. Remove the lid and cook for a further 30 minutes.

FREEZING INSTRUCTIONS Leave to cool completely, then transfer to a sealable freezerproof container, making sure the sausages are completely covered by the sauce. Freeze for up to 3 months. To serve, defrost in the refrigerator overnight, then cover loosely with cling film and reheat in a microwave on High for 2–3 minutes. Agitate, and heat for a further 2–3 minutes until piping hot. Leave to stand for 5 minutes before serving.

GOOD WITH Crisp green salad.

serves 8

prep 30 mins
• cook 2 hrs

Beef stew with orange and bay leaves

This attractive stew, which has a light sauce, is spiced with cinnamon and nutmeg to complement the flavour of the oranges.

INGREDIENTS

3 tbsp olive oil
1.35kg (3lb) stewing steak, cut into bite-sized pieces
salt and freshly ground black pepper
2 small glasses of dry white wine
3 bay leaves
1.7 litres (3 pints) hot vegetable stock
2 cinnamon sticks
pinch of nutmeg, freshly grated
2 x 400g cans chickpeas, drained and rinsed
2 oranges, peeled and sliced into rings
handful of coriander leaves, finely chopped, to serve

METHOD

1 Preheat the oven to 180°C (350°F/Gas 4). Heat the oil in a large flameproof casserole, add the meat, season with salt and pepper, and cook over a medium heat, stirring occasionally, for 10 minutes, or until brown on all sides. Carefully add the wine – it will spit – then stir the meat around the pan and allow the liquid to boil for a couple of minutes while the alcohol evaporates.

2 Add the bay leaves, then pour in the stock. Add the cinnamon and nutmeg, and season again with salt and pepper. Bring to the boil, add the chickpeas, then cover with a lid and put in the oven to cook for 1 hour. Add the oranges and cook for a further 30 minutes.

FREEZING INSTRUCTIONS Leave to cool completely, then transfer to a sealable freezerproof container, making sure the meat is well covered by the sauce. Freeze for up to 3 months. To serve, defrost overnight in the refrigerator, then reheat in a pan, topping up with a little hot water or hot stock. Simmer gently for 15 minutes, or until piping hot. Stir in some chopped coriander to serve.

GOOD WITH Fresh crusty bread.

serves 8

**prep 30 mins
• cook 1 hr
30 mins**

**large
flameproof
casserole**

Sausages with butter beans

This satisfying supper dish is particularly good on a cold winter evening.

INGREDIENTS
12 thick pork and herb sausages
1 tbsp olive oil
1 onion, sliced
1 celery stick, chopped
2 garlic cloves, crushed
75ml (2½fl oz) white wine
400g can chopped tomatoes
3 tbsp tomato ketchup
1 tsp paprika
salt and freshly ground black pepper
400g can butter beans, drained and rinsed
1 tbsp basil leaves or flat-leaf parsley,
    chopped, to serve

METHOD
1 Grill or fry the sausages until browned and cooked through.

2 Meanwhile, heat the oil in a saucepan and gently fry the onion, celery, and garlic, stirring frequently, until soft. Turn up the heat, add the wine and let it bubble for a few moments, then add the canned tomatoes with their juice. Stir in the ketchup and paprika, and season to taste with salt and pepper. Bring to the boil, reduce the heat, and simmer, uncovered, for about 20 minutes, or until thickened and reduced.

3 Stir in the butter beans and the cooked sausages, and simmer for a further 10 minutes. Serve immediately. Garnish with a sprinkling of chopped herbs.

FREEZING INSTRUCTIONS Leave to cool completely, then transfer to a sealable freezerproof container, making sure the sausages are completely covered by the sauce. Freeze for up to 3 months. To serve, defrost in the refrigerator overnight, then cover loosely with cling film and reheat in a microwave on High for 3–4 minutes. Agitate, and heat for a further 3–4 minutes until piping hot. Leave to stand for 5 minutes. Serve with a sprinkling of chopped fresh herbs.

GOOD WITH Creamy mashed potato or a mixture of carrot and potato mash.

serves 4

prep 10 mins
• cook 30 mins

Lamb, spinach, and chickpea hotpot

Hectic weeknights call for easy, wholesome dishes such as this one.

INGREDIENTS

675g (1½lb) lean lamb, cut into 2cm (¾in) dice
2 tbsp plain flour
1 tsp paprika
6 tbsp olive oil
2 large red onions, diced
6 garlic cloves, chopped
2 x 400g cans chickpeas, drained and rinsed
1 small glass of dry white wine
2 x 400g cans chopped tomatoes
salt and freshly ground black pepper
550g (1¼lb) baby leaf spinach

METHOD

1 Put the lamb, flour, and paprika in a mixing bowl and combine well. Heat the oil in a large heavy-based pan over a medium heat, add the onions, and cook, stirring frequently, for 5 minutes, or until soft and translucent. Add the lamb and cook, stirring occasionally, for 5 minutes, or until evenly browned. Stir in the garlic and chickpeas, and cook for 1 minute.

2 Pour in the wine and allow to boil for 3 minutes while the alcohol evaporates. Add the tomatoes, bring to the boil, then reduce the heat and simmer for 15 minutes. Season well with salt and pepper, stir in the spinach, and cook for 3 minutes.

FREEZING INSTRUCTIONS Leave to cool completely, then transfer to a sealable freezerproof container, making sure the meat is completely covered by the sauce. Freeze for up to 3 months. To serve, defrost overnight in the refrigerator, then transfer to a deep ovenproof dish, cover, and reheat in an oven preheated to 180°C (350°F/Gas 4) for 15–20 minutes, or until piping hot. Add a little hot water or hot stock if it starts to dry out. Alternatively, microwave on High for 3–4 minutes, stir, then heat for a further 3–4 minutes, or until piping hot. Leave to stand for 5 minutes before serving.

GOOD WITH Steamed or boiled rice.

serves 8

prep 25 mins
• cook 30 mins

healthy option

Game stew

Packs of mixed game can be bought ready-diced, cutting down on preparation time and producing a wonderfully rich-flavoured stew.

INGREDIENTS

1.35kg (3lb) (boned weight) mixed game, such as pheasant, venison, and duck, cut into bite-sized pieces
plain flour, to dust
salt and freshly ground black pepper
2 tbsp olive oil
2 tbsp brandy
2 onions, finely chopped

4 garlic cloves, grated or finely chopped
4 celery sticks, finely diced
4 carrots, finely diced
1 bouquet garni
550g (1¼lb) chestnut mushrooms, quartered
2 glasses of dry white wine
1 tbsp redcurrant jelly
1.4 litres (2½ pints) hot chicken stock

METHOD

1 Preheat the oven to 180°C (350°F/Gas 4). Dust the meat lightly with a little flour, then season well with salt and pepper. Heat half the oil in a large cast-iron pan, add the meat, and cook over a medium heat, stirring occasionally, for 6–8 minutes, or until browned on all sides. Remove with a slotted spoon and put to one side.

2 Add the brandy to the pan and stir to deglaze, then add the rest of the oil, if needed, and the onions and cook over a low heat for 6 minutes, or until soft. Stir in the garlic, celery, carrots, and bouquet garni and cook over a low heat, stirring occasionally, for 8 minutes, or until tender.

3 Stir in the mushrooms, then raise the heat, add the wine, and allow to boil for 2 minutes while the alcohol evaporates. Stir in the redcurrant jelly, then pour in the stock. Cover with a lid and put in the oven to cook for 1 hour, or until the meat is tender. Top up with hot water if needed.

FREEZING INSTRUCTIONS Leave to cool completely, then transfer to a sealable freezerproof container, making sure the meat is completely covered by sauce. Freeze for up to 3 months. To serve, defrost overnight in the refrigerator, then reheat gently in a pan. Simmer for 15–20 minutes, topping up with hot water if it starts to dry out, until piping hot.

GOOD WITH Creamy mashed potato.

serves 8

prep 30 mins
• cook 1 hr

large
cast-iron pan

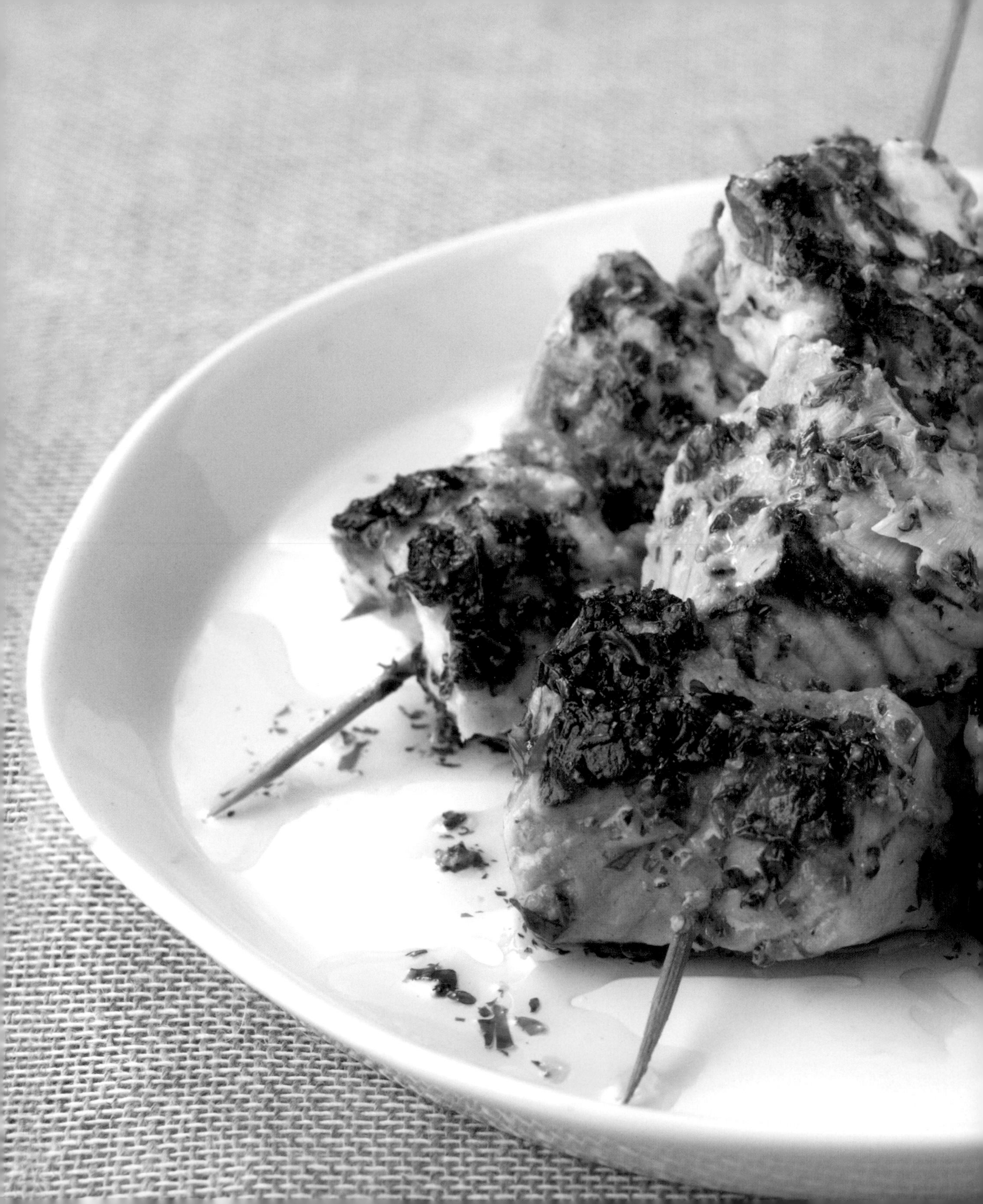

Swedish meatballs

Although regarded as Swedish, these are popular all over Scandinavia.

INGREDIENTS

60g (2oz) fresh breadcrumbs
120ml (4fl oz) double cream
60g (2oz) butter
1 small onion, finely chopped
200g (7oz) lean minced beef
200g (7oz) lean minced lamb
$\frac{1}{4}$ tsp freshly grated nutmeg
salt and freshly ground black pepper
1 egg, beaten

For the sauce

120ml (4fl oz) beef stock or lamb stock
200ml (7fl oz) double cream

METHOD

1 Put the breadcrumbs in a bowl, stir in the cream, and leave to soak. Meanwhile, heat 15g ($\frac{1}{2}$oz) of butter in a small pan, add the onion, and fry over a low heat until transparent but not brown. Set aside to cool.

2 Add the beef, lamb, and nutmeg to the breadcrumbs and season with salt and pepper. Stir in the onion and beaten egg until well combined. Cover with cling film and refrigerate for 1 hour.

3 With damp hands, shape the meat mixture firmly into golfball-sized balls. Place the meatballs on a large plate, cover with cling film, and refrigerate for 15 minutes.

4 Melt the remaining butter in a large frying pan over a medium heat and fry the meatballs in batches, turning gently, for 10 minutes, or until browned and cooked through. Remove with a slotted spoon, and drain on a plate lined with kitchen paper.

5 To make the sauce, drain any excess fat from the frying pan, pour in the stock and cream, and stir over a low heat until the sauce bubbles. Simmer for 2 minutes. Serve drizzled over the meatballs.

FREEZING INSTRUCTIONS Omit the sauce when freezing. Freeze the meatballs either uncooked or cooked and cooled. Transfer to a sealable freezerproof container and freeze for up to 3 months. To serve, defrost overnight in the refrigerator. If uncooked, fry as per Step 4. If cooked, reheat in a microwave on High for 2–3 minutes, agitate, and heat for a further 2–3 minutes until piping hot. Prepare the sauce as per Step 5 and drizzle over the meatballs.

GOOD WITH New potatoes and steamed broccoli.

serves 4

prep 30 mins,
plus chilling
• cook 20 mins

Spanish meatballs

These veal and pork meatballs, *albóndigas* in Spanish, are popular as tapas.

INGREDIENTS

750g (1lb 10oz) minced veal
250g (9oz) minced pork
2 garlic cloves, grated or finely chopped
115g (4oz) flat-leaf parsley, finely chopped
salt and freshly ground black pepper
$\frac{1}{2}$ tsp ground nutmeg
5 tbsp dry breadcrumbs
100ml (3$\frac{1}{2}$fl oz) milk

METHOD

1 Place the veal, pork, garlic, and parsley into a bowl, and mix together well. Season with pepper and nutmeg, and set aside.

2 Put the breadcrumbs in another bowl, pour in the milk, and set aside to soak.

3 Heat the olive oil in the casserole over a medium heat, and cook the onions, stirring, for 4–5 minutes, or until softened. Sprinkle in the flour and continue to cook for a further 1 minute. Pour in the wine, and season to taste with salt and pepper. Bring to a simmer, then reduce the heat and cook for 15 minutes, or until the sauce is reduced. Press the sauce through a sieve and return to the casserole, over a low heat.

4 Squeeze the excess milk from the breadcrumbs and add the crumbs to the meat with the eggs and 3 tbsp of the reduced sauce. Mix thoroughly, then roll the mixture into golfball-sized balls, and dust each with a little flour.

5 Heat the sunflower oil in a large frying pan. Working in batches, fry the meatballs, turning frequently, for 5 minutes, or until evenly browned. Remove them from the pan, drain on kitchen paper, and transfer to the casserole.

6 Poach the meatballs gently in the sauce for 20 minutes, or until the meatballs are no longer pink when cut in half. Serve warm, with the sauce poured over, and garnished with parsley.

FREEZING INSTRUCTIONS Leave to cool completely, then transfer to a sealable freezerproof container, making sure the meatballs are covered by the sauce. Freeze for up to 3 months. To serve, defrost in the refrigerator overnight, then reheat in a microwave on High for 2–3 minutes, agitate, and heat for a further 2–3 minutes. Leave to stand for 5 minutes. Serve with a sprinkling of chopped parsley.

GOOD WITH Crusty bread or with olive herbed mashed potatoes and green beans.

makes 48

prep 20 mins
• cook 1 hr

large
flameproof
casserole

Chicken schnitzels

A quick dish of Austrian origin, suitable for a family supper or a dinner party.

INGREDIENTS

45g (1½oz) plain flour
1 egg, beaten
about 60g (2oz) fine breadcrumbs
4 skinless boneless chicken breasts
salt and freshly ground black pepper
6 tbsp rapeseed oil
2 lemons, cut in half, to serve

METHOD

1 Put the flour in a shallow bowl, the egg in another bowl, and the breadcrumbs in a third bowl. Set aside.

2 Put the chicken breasts between 2 sheets of greaseproof paper and pound with a rolling pin until they are very thin. Season to taste with salt and pepper.

3 Coat the chicken in the flour, then in the beaten egg, and then in the breadcrumbs, pressing them evenly on to both sides. Place on a baking tray or plate in one layer and chill in the refrigerator, uncovered, for at least 30 minutes.

4 Heat 3 tbsp of the oil in a non-stick frying pan over a medium-high heat. Add 2 of the schnitzels and fry for 3 minutes on each side, or until golden brown and cooked through. Drain on kitchen paper and keep hot.

5 Add the remaining oil to the pan, and fry the remaining schnitzels, as before. Serve immediately, garnished with lemon halves, for squeezing over the schnitzels.

FREEZING INSTRUCTIONS Leave to cool, then freeze in a sealable freezerproof container for up to 3 months. To serve, defrost overnight in the refrigerator, then transfer to an oiled baking tray. Reheat in an oven preheated to 180°C (350°F/Gas 4) for 20–30 minutes until piping hot. Serve with lemon to squeeze over.

GOOD WITH Green beans or sautéed potatoes.

serves 4

prep 10 mins, plus chilling • cook 12 mins

Salmon fishcakes

These fishcakes could also be made with leftover roast salmon.

INGREDIENTS

450g (1lb) potatoes, cubed
900g (2lb) salmon fillets, skinned and boned
1 onion, halved
2–3 bay leaves
1 tsp black peppercorns
4 spring onions, finely chopped
2 tbsp horseradish cream
salt and freshly ground black pepper
grated zest and juice of 1 lemon
large handful of dill, chopped
pinch of cayenne pepper

For the coating

225g (8oz) fresh breadcrumbs
2 tbsp chives, chopped (optional)
2 tbsp flat-leaf parsley, chopped (optional)
plain flour, for coating
2 eggs, whisked
sunflower oil, for frying

METHOD

1 Place the potatoes in a saucepan of cold water and boil for 20 minutes, or until very tender. Drain and mash. Set aside.

2 Place the salmon in cold water with the onion, bay leaves, and peppercorns. Bring to the boil, simmer for 2 minutes, then turn off the heat and leave to cool for 20 minutes. Drain well, discarding the cooking liquids, and cool.

3 Flake the salmon into a large bowl. Fold in the cooled mashed potato and all the other fishcake ingredients. Mix well and shape into 12 round cakes. Chill for 1 hour, ideally, before coating.

4 Thoroughly mix the breadcrumbs with the herbs (if using). Put the flour, eggs, and breadcrumbs on separate plates and roll the salmon cakes in flour, then egg, then breadcrumbs.

5 Heat the sunflower oil in a frying pan and fry the fishcakes for 3–4 minutes on each side, or until crisp and hot in the middle. Drain on kitchen paper and serve while hot.

FREEZING INSTRUCTIONS Freeze the fishcakes either uncooked or cooked and cooled. Wrap each one individually in greaseproof paper then double wrap in cling film, or transfer to a sealable freezerproof container, and freeze for up to 3 months. To thaw, unwrap and place on a plate, or in the container, in the refrigerator to defrost overnight. If uncooked, fry as per Step 5. If cooked, transfer to an oiled baking tray and reheat in an oven preheated to 180°C (350°F/Gas 4) for 20–30 minutes until piping hot.

GOOD WITH Chunky chips, garden peas, and wedges of lemon.

serves 6

prep 30 mins,
plus cooling
and chilling
• cook 30 mins

Mixed fish kebabs

Use fish with a firm texture for these tasty kebabs.

INGREDIENTS
150g (5½oz) monkfish fillets, cut into cubes
150g (5½oz) salmon steaks or fillets, cut into cubes
150g (5½oz) tuna steaks, cut into cubes
grated zest and juice of 1 lime
2 garlic cloves, grated or finely chopped
handful of coriander leaves, finely chopped
5cm (2in) piece of fresh root ginger, finely chopped
splash of olive oil
salt and freshly ground black pepper

METHOD
1 Put all the ingredients in a large bowl and, using your hands, carefully combine everything until well mixed. Chill until needed.

2 Heat a ridged cast-iron grill pan until hot. Thread the fish on to the skewers in alternating pieces. Grill over a high heat for about 3 minutes on each side, turning only once during cooking. Serve hot.

FREEZING INSTRUCTIONS Freeze the kebabs uncooked, but only if the fish has not been frozen before. Prepare the recipe as in Step 1 and then thread on to skewers. Freeze in a sealable freezerproof container or freezer bags for up to 1 month. To serve, defrost overnight in the refrigerator, then cook on a hot ridged cast-iron grill pan for about 3 minutes on each side.

GOOD WITH Fresh green salad.

serves 4

prep 15 mins
• cook 6 mins

healthy option

soak the
skewers in cold
water for
at least 30 mins

ridged cast-iron
grill pan
• wooden
skewers

Pan-fried lamb with green chillies

This is an especially good dish to reheat and eat – its flavours improve when it is made in advance.

INGREDIENTS

1 tbsp olive oil
1 onion, finely chopped
1 bay leaf
pinch of cumin seeds
salt
2 garlic cloves, grated or finely chopped
1 green chilli, deseeded and finely chopped
900g (2lb) lean lamb, cut into bite-sized pieces
1 tbsp plain flour
600ml (1 pint) hot vegetable or chicken stock
3–4 green bird's-eye chillies, left whole
juice of $1/2$ lemon

METHOD

1 Heat the oil in a large deep sided frying pan. Add the onion, bay leaf, cumin seeds, and a pinch of salt, and sauté gently until soft. Stir through the garlic and chopped chilli, and sauté for a few seconds more.

2 Add the lamb, and brown on all sides, then stir through the flour. Pour in a little of the stock, increase the heat, and keep stirring.

3 Bring to the boil, then add the remaining stock and the whole bird's-eye chillies. Simmer for about 20 minutes until the lamb is cooked and the sauce has thickened. Stir in the lemon juice, and serve.

FREEZING INSTRUCTIONS Leave to cool completely, then transfer to a sealable freezerproof container, making sure the meat is completely covered by the sauce. Freeze for up to 3 months. To serve, defrost in the refrigerator overnight, then reheat in a microwave on High for 2–3 minutes, stir, and heat for a further 2–3 minutes. Leave to stand for 5 minutes before serving.

serves 4

prep 5 mins
• cook 30 mins

Chicken and chilli burgers

These zingy burgers are perfect for anyone who likes their chicken with a bit of spice.

INGREDIENTS

1 onion, peeled and quartered
4 skinless boneless chicken breast fillets
2 garlic cloves, peeled and halved
2 red chillies, deseeded
handful of coriander leaves, finely chopped
salt and freshly ground black pepper
1 tbsp plain flour
1 egg, lightly beaten

METHOD

1 Put the onion, chicken, garlic, chillies, and coriander in a food processor. Season with salt and pepper, and pulse until combined – be careful not to turn the mixture into a paste. Tip the mixture out into a bowl, and mix in the flour and egg.

2 Using your hands, scoop a small handful of the mixture, roll, then flatten into a burger. Repeat until all the mixture has been used. Chill for 30 minutes to firm up.

3 Grill the burgers under a medium heat for 8–10 minutes on each side until golden and cooked through. Serve sandwiched in burger buns.

FREEZING INSTRUCTIONS Freeze the burgers either uncooked or cooked and cooled. Layer them between sheets of greaseproof paper, then wrap in a plastic freezer bag and freeze for up to 3 months. To serve, remove from the freezer bag and defrost overnight in the refrigerator. If uncooked, grill as per Step 3. If cooked, reheat in a microwave on High for 2–3 minutes, turn, and heat for a further 2–3 minutes until piping hot. Leave to stand for 5 minutes before serving.

GOOD WITH Lemon mayonnaise and fresh tomato slices.

serves 4

prep 10 mins, plus chilling • cook 20 mins

healthy option

food processor

Fish fingers with chunky tartare sauce

Loved by old and young alike, fish fingers are a simple but delicious way to enjoy fresh fish.

INGREDIENTS
675g (1½lb) thick white fish fillets (loin works best),
   such as haddock, sustainable cod, or pollack, skinned
1–2 tbsp plain flour
1 egg, lightly beaten
115g (4oz) fresh breadcrumbs, toasted
60g (2oz) Parmesan cheese, finely grated
salt and freshly ground black pepper
3 tbsp tartare sauce
1 tsp capers, rinsed, drained, and chopped
3 gherkins, drained and finely chopped

METHOD
1 Preheat the oven to 200°C (400°F/Gas 6). Cut the fish fillets into thick even strips about 2.5cm (1in) wide – you should end up with about 20 "fingers".

2 Tip the flour and egg on to separate plates. Mix the breadcrumbs with the Parmesan, and season with salt and pepper. Dredge the fish in the flour, then dip in the egg to coat. Use the breadcrumb mixture to coat each of the fish fingers. Make sure that you coat them well, as it protects the fish while it's cooking.

3 Sit the fish fingers on a lightly oiled baking tray, and bake in the oven for 5–8 minutes on each side until golden and cooked through. (Alternatively, you can shallow-fry them in a little sunflower oil if you prefer).

4 Tip the tartare sauce into a bowl, and stir through the capers and gherkins. Serve with the hot fish fingers.

FREEZING INSTRUCTIONS Leave to cool completely, then layer between sheets of greaseproof paper, seal in a plastic freezer bag, and freeze for up to 3 months. To serve, remove from the freezer bag, defrost in the refrigerator overnight, then fry for a couple of minutes on each side until warmed through. Alternatively, reheat in a microwave on Medium for 1–2 minutes, turn, and heat for a further 1–2 minutes. Leave to stand for 5 minutes before serving with the tartare sauce. Don't freeze the tartare sauce but make it on the day you wish to serve the fish fingers.

GOOD WITH Chunky chips and peas or in a bread roll.

serves 4

prep 15 mins
• cook 10 mins

food processor

Seared herbed chicken with green herb sauce

The herbed crust seals in the juices, keeping the meat succulent.

INGREDIENTS

6 skinless boneless chicken breasts,
   about 175g (6oz) each
2 tbsp plain flour
350g (12oz) breadcrumbs
2 tbsp chopped thyme leaves
2 tbsp chopped flat-leaf parsley
175g (6oz) Parmesan cheese, finely grated
salt and freshly ground black pepper
2 eggs, lightly beaten
4 tbsp olive oil
4 tbsp sunflower oil

For the green herb sauce

2 tbsp white wine vinegar
2 egg yolks
1 egg
1 tbsp Dijon mustard
1 tbsp soft brown sugar or caster sugar
300ml (10fl oz) sunflower oil
20g ($^3/_4$oz) mixed fresh herbs, such
   as parsley, basil, dill, watercress, coriander,
   and chives, roughly chopped
salt and freshly ground black pepper

METHOD

1 For the sauce, place the vinegar, yolks, egg, mustard, and sugar into a food processor or blender, then gradually add the oil with the motor running to form a thick and creamy mayonnaise. Once all the oil has been added, blend in the herbs. Season to taste with salt and pepper, and set aside.

2 Cut the chicken breasts into halves and dust lightly with flour. Place the breadcrumbs in a bowl with the thyme, parsley, and Parmesan, season to taste with salt and pepper, and mix well. Coat the chicken in the egg, then the breadcrumbs.

3 Heat the frying pan with some of each oil. Fry the chicken in 2–3 batches for 5 minutes on each side, or until crisp and golden, adding more oil with each batch. Drain, then serve with the green herb sauce.

FREEZING INSTRUCTIONS Leave to cool completely, then wrap in greaseproof paper and a double wrapping of cling film, and freeze for up to 2 months. To serve, remove from the wrapping and defrost in the refrigerator overnight. Reheat on an oiled baking tray in an oven preheated to 180°C (350°F/Gas 4) for 40 minutes, or until piping hot. Alternatively, reheat in a microwave on High for 3–4 minutes, turn, and heat for a further 3–4 minutes. Leave to stand for 5 minutes before serving. Do not freeze the green herb sauce but make it fresh on the day you wish to serve the chicken.

serves 6

prep 20 mins
• cook 20–30 mins

food processor
or blender

Thai crab cakes

These make a delicious lunch or light supper dish served with rice noodles.

INGREDIENTS

500g (1lb 2oz) white crabmeat
115g (4oz) green beans, trimmed and finely chopped
1 green chilli or red chilli, deseeded and very finely chopped
1 tsp lemongrass purée
finely grated zest of 1 lime
1 tbsp Thai fish sauce, such as nam pla
1 tbsp Chinese chives or garlic chives, finely chopped
1 egg white, lightly beaten
plain flour, to dust
vegetable oil, for deep-frying

METHOD

1 Flake the crabmeat into a bowl, picking it over carefully to remove any small, sharp pieces of shell. Add the green beans, chilli, lemongrass purée, lime zest, fish sauce, and chives, and mix.

2 Add the egg white, stirring to bind the mixture together. Dust your hands with flour and shape the mixture into 20 small balls. Flatten them slightly into round cakes, place on a plate or board, spaced slightly apart so they don't stick together and chill for 1 hour, or until firm.

3 In a large, deep frying pan, heat the oil to 160°C (325°F). Dust the crab cakes with flour and deep-fry them in batches for 3 minutes, or until golden. Drain on a plate lined with kitchen paper and serve warm.

FREEZING INSTRUCTIONS Leave to cool completely, then layer between sheets of greaseproof paper, seal in a plastic freezer bag, and freeze for up to 1 month. To serve, remove from the freezer bag and defrost in the refrigerator overnight. Reheat in a microwave on Medium for 1–2 minutes, turn, and heat for a further 1–2 minutes until piping hot. Leave to stand for 5 minutes before serving.

GOOD WITH Spicy dipping sauce and a Thai noodle salad, or broken over a leafy green salad.

makes 20

prep 30 mins,
plus chilling
• cook 20 mins

Stuffed aubergines

A popular Turkish meze, *Imam Bayildi* are cold and spicy stuffed aubergines.

INGREDIENTS

4 aubergines
6 tbsp olive oil
2 large onions, finely sliced
3 garlic cloves, crushed
1 tbsp ground coriander
1 tbsp ground cumin
1 tsp ground turmeric
$\frac{1}{2}$ tsp ground cardamom
2 x 400g cans chopped tomatoes
85g (3oz) sultanas
2 tbsp coriander leaves, chopped
1 tbsp mint leaves, chopped
1 tbsp flat-leaf parsley, chopped

METHOD

1 Preheat the oven to 180°C (350°F/Gas 4). Cut the aubergines in half lengthways, and score the flesh in a criss-cross pattern using a sharp knife.

2 Brush the aubergine flesh with 4 tbsp of oil, and place the halves, cut-sides up, in a roasting tin. Bake for 30–35 minutes, or until the flesh is tender.

3 Leave the aubergine halves to cool, then scoop out and chop the flesh. Take care not to split the skins, and leave a thin layer of flesh in place to support them.

4 Heat the rest of the oil in a large, heavy pan, and cook the onion and garlic over a medium-low heat until softened. Add the spices and fry until they smell fragrant, stirring occasionally.

5 Stir in the tomatoes, bring to the boil, then reduce the heat and simmer for 30 minutes, or until the mixture is reduced, stirring occasionally. Add the sultanas and aubergine flesh and cook, stirring, for a further 10 minutes, or until heated though. Leave to cool, then stir in the coriander, mint, and parsley.

6 Spoon the mixture into the aubergine shells and chill for at least 3 hours, or overnight if possible before serving cold.

FREEZING INSTRUCTIONS Once filled, leave to cool completely and transfer to a sealable freezerproof container. Freeze for up to 1 month. To serve, defrost in the refrigerator overnight, then bring to room temperature before serving.

GOOD WITH A herb salad and Greek yogurt.

serves 4

prep 20 mins,
plus cooling
and chilling
• cook 1 hr
10 mins

healthy option

chill for at
least 3 hrs, or
overnight

Lamb and mint burgers

Fresh ginger and garlic add a twist to this classic flavour combination.

INGREDIENTS

1 tbsp olive oil
knob of butter
1 onion, finely chopped
2 garlic cloves, grated or finely chopped
2.5cm (1in) piece of fresh root ginger, grated
salt and freshly ground black pepper
675g (1½lb) lamb mince
handful of fresh mint leaves, finely chopped
vegetable oil, for frying

METHOD

1 In a large frying pan, heat the oil and butter over a low heat. Add the onion, and sweat for about 5 minutes until soft. Add the garlic, ginger, and some salt and pepper. Remove from the heat, and allow to cool.

2 Put the lamb mince in a large bowl, then tip in the cooled onion mixture and the mint. Season again, then mix together until well combined – this is best done using your hands. Roll large balls of the mixture together, and flatten to make burgers. Sit the burgers on a plate, and chill in the refrigerator to firm, if time permits.

3 Shallow-fry the burgers, a few at a time, in a little hot vegetable oil. Fry for 5–6 minutes on each side until cooked through and no longer pink. Alternatively, grill on a hot griddle, ridged cast-iron grill pan, or barbecue. Serve hot.

FREEZING INSTRUCTIONS Freeze the burgers either uncooked or cooked and cooled. Layer them between sheets of greaseproof paper, then seal in a plastic freezer bag and freeze for up to 3 months. To serve, remove from the freezer bag and defrost overnight in the refrigerator. If uncooked, cook as per Step 3. If cooked, reheat in a microwave on High for 2–3 minutes, turn, and heat for a further 2–3 minutes until piping hot. Leave to stand for 5 minutes before serving.

GOOD WITH Roasted butternut squash and wild rocket leaves.

serves 4

**prep 10 mins,
plus chilling
• cook 20 mins**

Aubergine parmigiana

This is one of Italy's most popular dishes and a great choice for vegetarians.

INGREDIENTS

2 large eggs
salt and freshly ground black pepper
45g (1$\frac{1}{2}$oz) plain white flour
2 aubergines, thinly sliced lengthways
4 tbsp sunflower oil
600ml (1 pint) passata
60g (2oz) Parmesan cheese, grated
1 bunch of basil, leaves torn (reserve a few leaves, to garnish)
300g (10oz) mozzarella, sliced

METHOD

1 Preheat the oven to 160°C (325°F/Gas 3). Beat the eggs in a shallow bowl and season with salt and pepper. Put the flour on a plate. Coat an aubergine slice in the flour, shaking off the excess, then tip it into the egg and let the excess drip back into the bowl. Repeat with the remaining slices.

2 Heat the oil in a large frying pan over a medium heat. Working in batches if necessary, fry the aubergine slices for 5 minutes on each side, or until golden. Drain well on kitchen paper, then continue until all the slices are fried.

3 Layer the passata, aubergine slices, Parmesan, basil leaves, and mozzarella in a shallow, ovenproof serving dish. Continue layering until all the ingredients are used, finishing with a layer of passata and the mozzarella on top. Season to taste with salt and pepper.

4 Place the dish on a baking tray and bake for 30 minutes, or until the sauce is bubbling and the mozzarella has melted. Top with extra basil leaves and serve hot.

FREEZING INSTRUCTIONS Assemble in a freezerproof baking dish. Leave to cool completely, then double wrap in cling film and freeze for up to 3 months. To serve, defrost in its container in the refrigerator overnight, remove the cling film and reheat in an oven preheated to 180°C (350°F/Gas 4) for 30–40 minutes, or until piping hot. Alternatively, reheat portions in a microwave on Medium for 2–3 minutes, agitate, and heat for a further 2–3 minutes until piping hot. Leave to stand for 5 minutes before serving.

GOOD WITH A simple salad.

serves 4

prep 40 mins
• cook 30 mins

Moussaka

This recipe makes individual servings, which are easier to freeze.

INGREDIENTS

2 large aubergines, cut into 5mm (¼in) slices
salt and freshly ground black pepper
5 tbsp olive oil
1 large onion, chopped
450g (1lb) lean lamb mince
100ml (3½fl oz) red wine
400g can chopped tomatoes
1 tsp sugar
100ml (3½fl oz) lamb stock
2 tsp dried oregano

450g (1lb) potatoes, cut into 5mm (¼in) slices
4 tbsp Parmesan cheese
4 tbsp dried breadcrumbs

For the topping

200g (7oz) Greek strained yogurt
3 large eggs
1 tbsp cornflour
115g (4oz) curd cheese
60g (2oz) feta cheese, crumbled

METHOD

1 Spread out the aubergine slices on a plate, sprinkle liberally with salt, and leave to stand for 30 minutes. Tip the slices into a colander, rinse thoroughly under cold water, drain, and pat dry.

2 Heat 2 tbsp of oil in a large deep frying pan, add the onion, and cook over a low heat, stirring often, until softened. Increase the heat and fry the mince until starting to brown, breaking up any clumps with a spoon.

3 Add the wine, allow to bubble for 1–2 minutes, then add the tomatoes, sugar, stock, and 1 tsp of oregano, and season to taste with salt and pepper. Simmer, uncovered, for 30 minutes, or until most of the liquid in the pan has evaporated and the meat sauce is quite thick.

4 Meanwhile, brush the aubergine slices with the remaining oil and grill in batches until softened and golden on both sides. Boil the potato slices in a saucepan of water for 10–15 minutes, or until just tender. Drain.

5 To make the topping, whisk the yogurt, eggs, and cornflour together until smooth, then whisk in the curd and feta.

6 Preheat the oven to 180°C (350°F/Gas 4). Layer the aubergine slices with the meat mixture into the baking dishes, starting with aubergine and finishing with meat. Arrange the potato slices on top in an overlapping layer.

7 Spread the topping to cover the potatoes completely, scatter with Parmesan, breadcrumbs, and the remaining oregano, and bake for 45 minutes, or until golden brown and bubbling.

FREEZING INSTRUCTIONS Leave the moussakas to cool completely in their dishes, then double wrap in cling film and freeze for up to 3 months. To serve, defrost in their dishes in the refrigerator overnight, remove the cling film, cover with foil, and reheat in an oven preheated to 180°C (350°F/Gas 4) for 30–40 minutes, or until piping hot.

serves 4

prep 30 mins,
plus standing
• cook 1 hr
30 mins

4 x 8–10cm
(3½–4in)
ovenproof
casserole dishes

Coquilles St Jacques

This seafood classic makes an impressive and elegant main course.

INGREDIENTS

8 scallops, white muscle and
   orange roe removed
6 tbsp medium white wine
1 bay leaf
7.5cm (3in) piece of celery
4 black peppercorns
small sprig of thyme
salt and freshly ground black pepper
225g (8oz) button mushrooms
juice of 1/2 lemon
60g (2oz) butter
1 tbsp plain flour

6 tbsp double cream or crème fraîche
50g (1³/₄oz) Gruyère cheese or
   Emmental cheese, grated

For the piped potatoes

450g (1lb) floury potatoes, peeled
   and cut into 2–3 pieces
30g (1oz) butter
large pinch of grated nutmeg
salt and freshly ground black pepper
3 egg yolks

METHOD

1 Boil the potatoes, then mash with the butter, nutmeg, and seasoning to taste. Beat the mash over a low heat until fluffy, then remove from the heat and beat in the egg yolks. Allow to cool, spoon into a piping bag, and pipe a generous border of potato around the edges of each shell or ramekin.

2 Preheat the oven to 220°C (425°F/Gas 7). Place the scallops in a small saucepan, add 150ml (5fl oz) water, the wine, bay leaf, celery, peppercorns, thyme, and a good pinch of salt. Bring slowly to the boil, cover, and simmer gently for 1–2 minutes, or until the scallops just whiten. Transfer them to a bowl, strain the liquid, reserve to make the sauce, and discard the vegetables.

3 Gently cook the mushrooms with the lemon juice, 2 tbsp of water, and salt and pepper to taste in a covered pan for 5–7 minutes, or until tender. If any liquid remains, simmer, uncovered, until it has evaporated. Add the mushrooms to the scallops.

4 Melt the butter in a pan. Stir in the flour, and cook gently for 1 minute, stirring constantly. Remove from the heat, and gradually stir in the reserved liquid. Slowly bring to the boil, and continue to cook, stirring constantly, until thickened. Season to taste with salt and pepper, and simmer gently for 4–5 minutes. Reduce the heat and stir in the cream, and half the cheese. Cut each cooked scallop into 2 or 3 pieces, and stir into the sauce with the mushrooms.

5 Spoon the mixture into each shell or ramekin, and sprinkle the remaining cheese on top. Bake for about 15 minutes, or until the sauce and potatoes are golden, and serve.

FREEZING INSTRUCTIONS Assemble in freezerproof dishes. Leave to cool, then double wrap in cling film and freeze for up to 3 months. To serve, defrost in the container in the refrigerator overnight, remove the cling film, and reheat in a microwave on Medium for 2–3 minutes, agitate, and heat for a further 2–3 minutes until piping hot.

serves 4

prep 20 mins
• cook 50 mins

4 scallop shells
or 4 ramekins
• piping bag

Shepherd's pie

Traditionally, this pie was a use for leftover roast meat and potatoes, but is now more commonly made with minced lamb.

INGREDIENTS

1.1kg (2½lb) floury potatoes
large knob of butter
salt and freshly ground black pepper
6 tbsp olive oil
3 large onions, diced
4 large carrots, diced
1.1kg (2½lb) lamb mince
6 garlic cloves, chopped
2 tsp dried oregano
3 x 400g cans chopped tomatoes
250g (9oz) frozen peas

METHOD

1 Preheated the oven to 180°C (350°F/Gas 4). Put the potatoes in a pan of boiling salted water and cook for 15 minutes, or until soft. Drain, then mash well. Add the butter and mash again until creamy. Season with salt and pepper, then put to one side.

2 Meanwhile, heat the oil in a large heavy-based pan over a medium heat, add the onions and carrots and cook for 5 minutes, or until the onions are starting to soften. Add the lamb and cook, stirring constantly, for 10 minutes, or until no longer pink. Add the garlic and oregano, cook for 1 minute, then stir in the tomatoes and bring to the boil.

3 Add the peas, season well with salt and pepper, then bring to the boil before lowering the heat. Simmer for 20 minutes, stirring occasionally. Pour a layer of the lamb sauce into 2 large tin-foil dishes, or individual serving dishes, and top with the mashed potato.

4 Place the dishes in the oven and bake for 25 minutes, or until brown on top and piping hot.

FREEZING INSTRUCTIONS Assemble in freezerproof baking dishes. Leave to cool completely, then double wrap in cling film and freeze for up to 3 months. To serve, defrost in the container in the refrigerator overnight, and reheat in a microwave on High for 3–4 minutes, agitate, and heat for a further 3–4 minutes until piping hot. Leave to stand for 5 minutes before serving.

GOOD WITH A green salad or minted peas.

serves 8

prep 30 mins
• cook 45 mins

Vegetarian leek and mushroom lasagne

Grated mushrooms add a meaty texture and chillies a pleasant heat to this dish.

INGREDIENTS

6 tbsp olive oil
4 large leeks, cut into 5mm (¼in) slices
550g (1¼lb) chestnut mushrooms, sliced
250g (9oz) chestnut mushrooms, grated
2–3 red chillies, deseeded and finely chopped
6 garlic cloves, chopped
150ml (5fl oz) dry white wine
small handful of thyme leaves

2 tbsp plain flour
900ml (1½ pints) milk
350g (12oz) Cheddar cheese, grated
6 tomatoes, roughly chopped,
   plus 1 extra, sliced
salt and freshly ground black pepper
450g (1lb) lasagne sheets

METHOD

1 Preheat the oven to 180°C (350°F/Gas 4). Heat the oil in a large heavy-based pan, add the leeks, and cook over a low heat, stirring frequently, for 5 minutes, or until starting to soften. Stir in the mushrooms and cook, stirring frequently, for 5 minutes, or until they release their juices. Add the chillies and garlic, and cook for 1 minute. Pour in the wine, raise the heat, and boil for 3 minutes while the alcohol evaporates.

2 Stir in the thyme, then add the flour and mix well. Add a little of the milk, mix well, then add the rest of the milk and cook for 5 minutes, stirring frequently. Add almost all the cheese (reserve some for the topping), remove from the heat, and combine well. Add the chopped tomatoes and season well with salt and pepper.

3 Put a 1cm (½in) layer of the mixture in the bottom of a large ovenproof dish, then cover evenly with a layer of the lasagne sheets. Pour in another layer of sauce and cover with lasagne. Repeat the process until all the sauce is used up – you need to finish with a layer of sauce. Top with the remaining cheese and the sliced tomato.

4 Place the dish in the oven for 30 minutes, or until browning on top and piping hot.

FREEZING INSTRUCTIONS Assemble in a freezerproof baking dish. Leave to cool completely, then double wrap in cling film and freeze for up to 3 months. To serve, defrost in its container in the refrigerator overnight, remove the cling film, cover with foil, and reheat in an oven preheated to 180°C (350°F/Gas 4) for 30–40 minutes, or until piping hot. Alternatively, reheat portions in a microwave on Medium for 2–3 minutes, agitate, and heat for a further 2–3 minutes until piping hot. Leave to stand for 5 minutes before serving.

serves 8

prep 25 mins
• cook 50 mins

Spinach and mushroom pancakes

These savoury filled pancakes make a perfect mid-week meal.

INGREDIENTS

115g (4oz) plain flour
1 egg
1 egg yolk
300ml (10fl oz) milk
1 tbsp light olive oil or melted butter,
   plus extra for frying

For the filling

2 tbsp light olive oil or melted butter
200g (7oz) mushrooms, chopped

pinch of grated nutmeg
250g (9oz) cooked spinach, chopped
900ml (1½ pints) béchamel sauce
85g (3oz) grated Cheddar cheese
½ tsp dry mustard
salt and freshly ground black pepper
2 tomatoes, sliced
3 tbsp grated Parmesan cheese

METHOD

1 To make the pancakes, sift the flour into a bowl and make a well in the centre. Add the egg and egg yolk, plus a little of the milk, and whisk until smooth. Whisk in the rest of the milk and 1 tbsp of oil or melted butter. Pour into a jug.

2 Lightly grease a 15–18cm (6–7in) heavy frying pan, add a little of the batter mix, and swirl so it coats the base of the pan in a thin layer. Cook until set and golden underneath, then flip the pancake over to cook the other side. Slide out of the pan on to a plate, then repeat with the remaining mixture to make 11 more pancakes, re-greasing the pan as necessary.

3 To make the filling, heat 2 tbsp of oil or melted butter in a frying pan and fry the mushrooms until tender. Drain well. Transfer to a bowl and add the nutmeg, spinach, and 4 tbsp of béchamel sauce.

4 Preheat the oven to 190°C (375°F/Gas 5). Divide the filling between the pancakes, roll up, and arrange in a shallow ovenproof dish.

5 Stir the cheese and mustard into the rest of the béchamel sauce, season with salt and pepper, and spoon over the pancakes in an even layer. Arrange the tomato slices on top and scatter with the grated Parmesan. Bake for 30 minutes. Serve hot.

FREEZING INSTRUCTIONS Freeze this dish uncooked. Assemble in a freezerproof baking dish, double wrap in cling film and freeze for up to 3 months. To serve, defrost overnight in the refrigerator, remove the cling film, cover with foil, and reheat in an oven preheated to 180°C (350°F/Gas 4) for 30–40 minutes, or until piping hot.

serves 4

prep 30 mins
• cook 1 hr
10 mins

15–18cm (6–7in)
heavy
frying pan

Cheesy potato and mushroom gratin

Both vegetarians and non-vegetarians will love this hearty, homely bake.

INGREDIENTS
knob of butter
125g (4½oz) chestnut or button mushrooms, sliced
2 garlic cloves, grated or finely chopped
a few sprigs of thyme, leaves picked
900g (2lb) potatoes, peeled and thinly sliced
125g (4½oz) Gruyère cheese, grated
salt and freshly ground black pepper

METHOD
1 Preheat the oven to 200°C (400°F/Gas 6). Melt the butter in a pan, then add the mushrooms and cook for a few minutes until soft. Add the garlic and thyme, and cook for a minute more.

2 Arrange a layer of potatoes in the bottom of an ovenproof dish, then layer with some of the cheese and mushrooms. Keep layering until you have used all of the ingredients, finishing with a layer of potato and a sprinkling of cheese on top. Season with a pinch of salt and pepper as you go.

3 Bake in the oven for 25 minutes until golden and simmering.

FREEZING INSTRUCTIONS Assemble in a freezerproof baking dish. Leave to cool completely, then double wrap in cling film and freeze for up to 3 months. To serve, defrost in its container in the refrigerator overnight, remove the cling film, and reheat in a microwave on Medium for 3–4 minutes, agitate, and heat for a further 3–4 minutes until piping hot. Leave to stand for 5 minutes before serving.

GOOD WITH A crisp green salad.

serves 4

prep 10 mins
• cook 30 mins

Vegetarian moussaka

A healthier, but equally delicious, take on this famous Greek dish.

INGREDIENTS

1 tbsp olive oil
1 onion, finely chopped
salt and freshly ground black pepper
1 tsp dried mint
3 tsp dried oregano
400g can aduki beans, drained and rinsed
700g jar passata
25g (scant 1oz) pine nuts
250ml (9fl oz) Greek-style yogurt
1 egg, lightly beaten

METHOD

1 Preheat the oven to 200°C (400°F/Gas 6). Heat the oil in a saucepan over a low heat. Add the onion and a pinch of salt, and sweat gently for about 5 minutes until soft. Sprinkle over the dried mint and 1 tsp of the dried oregano, and stir through.

2 Add the aduki beans, passata, and pine nuts, and bring to the boil. Reduce the heat to low, and simmer gently for 15–20 minutes until thickened. Season well with salt and pepper.

3 Spoon the bean mixture into an ovenproof dish. Mix together the yogurt, egg, and remaining 2 tsp of dried oregano. Spoon evenly over the top of the bean mixture. Bake in the oven for 15–20 minutes, until the top is golden, puffed, and set. Serve hot.

FREEZING INSTRUCTIONS Assemble in a freezerproof baking dish. Leave to cool completely, then double wrap in cling film and freeze for up to 3 months. To serve, defrost in its container in the refrigerator overnight, remove the cling film, cover with foil, and reheat in an oven preheated to 180°C (350°F/Gas 4) for 30–50 minutes, or until piping hot.

GOOD WITH A green salad.

serves 4

prep 15 mins
• cook 45 mins

healthy option

Shepherdless pie

Aduki beans make a satisfying vegetarian version of this potato-topped pie.

INGREDIENTS

675g (1½lb) floury potatoes,
   peeled and quartered
2 knobs of butter
1 tbsp olive oil
1 onion, finely chopped
1 bay leaf
3 celery sticks, finely chopped
3 carrots, finely chopped

200g (7oz) chestnut mushrooms,
   roughly chopped
handful of thyme sprigs, leaves picked
splash of dark soy sauce
400g can aduki beans, drained and rinsed
salt and freshly ground black pepper
150ml (5fl oz) hot vegetable stock

METHOD

1 Preheat the oven to 200°C (400°F/Gas 6). To make the mash topping, boil the potatoes in a pan of salted water for 15–20 minutes until soft. Drain, then mash. Add a knob of butter, and mash again. Set aside.

2 Meanwhile, heat the oil in a large frying pan over a low heat. Add the onion, bay leaf, and a pinch of salt, and sweat for about 5 minutes until the onion is soft. Now add the celery and carrot, and continue to sweat gently for a further 5 minutes.

3 Pulse the mushrooms in a food processor until broken down – you want them shredded, but not mushy. Add these to the pan, along with the thyme leaves and soy sauce, and cook for a further 5–10 minutes until the mushrooms begin to release their juices. Add the aduki beans, and season well with salt and pepper. Pour over the stock, bring to the boil, reduce the heat slightly, and simmer gently for 5 minutes.

4 Tip into an ovenproof dish, and top with the reserved mashed potato. Dot with butter, and bake in the oven until the top is starting to become crisp and golden. Serve hot.

FREEZING INSTRUCTIONS Assemble in a freezerproof baking dish. Leave to cool completely, then double wrap in cling film and freeze for up to 3 months. To serve, defrost in its container in the refrigerator overnight, and reheat in a microwave on Medium for 3–4 minutes, agitate, and heat for a further 3–4 minutes until piping hot. Leave to stand for 5 minutes before serving.

serves 4

**prep 15 mins
• cook 30 mins**

healthy option

food processor

Haddock mornay

A layer of spinach under poached haddock makes this a colourful one-pot meal.

INGREDIENTS
675g (1½lb) haddock fillet, skinned
  and cut into 4 equal pieces
150ml (5fl oz) fish stock or water
300ml (10fl oz) milk
45g (1½oz) butter, plus extra for greasing
45g (1½oz) plain flour
115g (4oz) Cheddar cheese, grated
salt and freshly ground black pepper
250g (9oz) spinach, chopped
pinch of grated nutmeg
60g (2oz) fresh wholemeal breadcrumbs
2 tbsp flat-leaf parsley, chopped
60g (2oz) grated Parmesan cheese

METHOD
1 Place the haddock in a deep frying pan and pour the stock and milk over. Slowly bring to the boil, then lower the heat, cover, and simmer for 6–8 minutes, or until the fish is cooked. Lift the fish from the pan and keep warm, reserving the poaching liquid.

2 Melt the butter in a saucepan and stir in the flour until smooth. Cook for 1 minute, then gradually whisk or stir in the poaching liquid until evenly combined. Stir over the heat until the sauce is thickened and smooth. Stir in the Cheddar until melted, then season to taste with salt and pepper. Remove from the heat.

3 Put the spinach in a saucepan, cover, and cook over a low heat for 1 minute, or until the leaves have wilted. Season with the nutmeg, transfer to a greased, shallow, ovenproof dish, and spread it out in an even layer. Preheat the grill.

4 Place the poached haddock on the spinach and pour the cheese sauce over the fish. Mix together the breadcrumbs, parsley, and Parmesan, and sprinkle over the sauce. Place the dish under the grill until the topping is golden.

FREEZING INSTRUCTIONS Assemble in a freezerproof baking dish. Leave to cool completely, then double wrap in cling film and freeze for up to 3 months. To serve, defrost in its container in the refrigerator overnight, and reheat in a microwave on Medium for 3–4 minutes, agitate, and heat for a further 3–4 minutes until piping hot. Leave to stand for 5 minutes before serving.

serves 4

prep 25 mins
• cook 25 mins

Make basic pizza dough

A quick dough mixture using dried yeast – the quantities given here make 4 thin-crust Italian-style pizzas.

1 Sift 500g (1lb 2oz) of "00" or strong white flour into a bowl, add a pinch of salt, and a 7g sachet of dried yeast. Slowly add 360ml (12fl oz) of warm water and mix until it comes together. Add 60ml (2fl oz) of olive oil, and mix to a soft dough.

2 Place the dough on a floured surface, and knead firmly, using the heel of your hand, folding the dough over as you go. Continue kneading for about 10 minutes, until it becomes soft and spongy.

3 Put the dough in a bowl, cover with cling film or a tea towel, and leave in a warm place (try leaving the bowl on a hob above a preheated oven) for 30–40 minutes, or until it has doubled in size.

4 Place the dough on a floured surface, and knead with your knuckles for a few minutes. Divide the dough into 4 and roll each piece out thinly to a size of about 25cm (10in) in diameter.

Make shortcrust pastry

Baked shortcrust pastry has a crisp and firm, but light, texture. This is the one to start with for anyone new to pastry-making.

1 Sift 175g (6oz) plain flour and a pinch of salt into a large bowl. Add 85g (3oz) chilled, diced butter, margarine, or other fat. Lightly stir to coat the butter in the flour

2 Quickly and lightly rub the butter or margarine into the flour with your fingertips until the mixture resembles coarse breadcrumbs. Try to incorporate all the flour.

3 Sprinkle over 2 tbsp of iced water and stir with a wooden spoon or use your hands to gently mix until the dough comes together (the less you handle the dough, the lighter the pastry will be).

4 Shape the dough into a ball, wrap it in cling film, and chill for at least 30 minutes before using. The gluten and flour will relax during chilling, helping to prevent the dough from shrinking in the hot oven.

Line a tart tin

Once your pastry dough is made, and has had time to chill and relax, follow these steps to line any size and shape of tin.

1 Lightly flour a work surface, then roll out the chilled pastry to a circle that is about 5cm (2in) wider than the tart tin. The pastry should be even and fairly thin.

2 Carefully drape the pastry over a rolling pin and gently lay it over the tart tin, so the pastry hangs over the edge on all sides.

3 Gently ease the pastry into the sides of the tin using your fingertips or knuckles, being careful not to tear it.

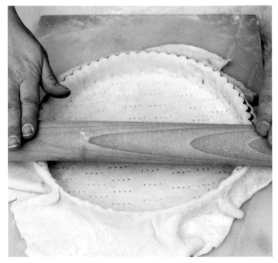

4 Prick the base all over with a fork, then roll a rolling pin over the top of the tin to cut away the excess pastry. Place in the refrigerator to chill for 30 minutes before baking.

Bake pastry blind

A pastry case for a tart or pie must be pre-cooked if its filling will not be baked or baked only for a short time.

1 Fit the pastry dough in the tart tin (see opposite) and ensure that you prick the bottom thoroughly with a fork. This will allow trapped air to escape during baking, helping to prevent soggy pastry.

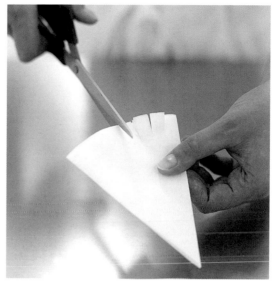

2 Cut out a circle of greaseproof paper, just slightly larger than the tin. Fold the paper in half 3 times to make a triangular shape and clip the edges at regular intervals with scissors.

3 Place the paper circle into the tin and fill it with an even layer of ceramic or metal baking beans. Bake at 180°C (350°F/ Gas 4) for 15–20 minutes – it will be partially baked.

4 When cool enough to handle, remove the beans and greaseproof paper. For fully baked pastry, return the pastry to the oven for a further 5–8 minutes, or until golden.

Pizza with tomatoes, olives, and capers

Passata, or sieved tomatoes, is ideal for pizza bases, but if you cannot get any, try blending canned tomatoes instead.

INGREDIENTS

1 quantity basic pizza dough (see page 156)
flour, to dust
semolina, for sprinkling
2–3 tbsp passata
3 tomatoes, sliced
handful of pitted black olives
1–2 tsp capers, rinsed
freshly ground black pepper

METHOD

1 Preheat the oven to its highest setting. Very lightly oil a baking tray and put it in the oven to get hot.

2 Place the dough on a floured surface and use a rolling pin to roll it out as thin as you can – about 25–30cm (10–12in) in diameter. Sprinkle the hot baking tray with semolina and transfer the dough on to it.

3 Spoon the passata on the pizza base, using the back of the spoon to smooth it out evenly. Top with the tomato slices, then arrange the olives and capers on top. Bake for 10–15 minutes, or until the crust and base are crisp and golden. Season with pepper and serve.

FREEZING INSTRUCTIONS Leave to cool completely, then double wrap in cling film and freeze for up to 1 month. To serve, defrost overnight in the refrigerator, then slice, and reheat in a microwave on Medium for 1–2 minutes, turn, and heat for 1–2 minutes more, or until piping hot. Leave to stand for 5 minutes before serving.

serves 4

prep 10 mins, plus making the dough • cook 15 mins

Pissaladière

This pizza got its name from *pissala*, a paste made from anchovies.

INGREDIENTS

225g (8oz) strong white flour,
  plus extra for dusting
salt and freshly ground black pepper
1 tsp soft brown sugar
1 tsp easy-blend dried yeast
1 tbsp olive oil

For the topping

4 tbsp olive oil
900g (2lb) onions, finely sliced
3 garlic cloves
sprig of thyme
1 tsp herbes de Provence (dry mix of thyme,
  basil, rosemary, and oregano)
1 bay leaf
100g jar anchovies in oil
12 black pitted Niçoise olives, or Italian olives
freshly ground black pepper

METHOD

1 For the base, combine the flour, 1 tsp of salt, and pepper to taste in a large bowl. Pour 150ml (5fl oz) tepid water into a separate bowl, and use a fork to whisk in the sugar, then the yeast. Set aside for 10 minutes to froth, then pour into the flour with the olive oil.

2 Mix to form a dough, adding a further 2 tbsp of tepid water, if the mixture looks too dry. Turn the dough out on to a floured board, and knead for 10 minutes, or until smooth and elastic. Shape the dough into a ball, return to the bowl, and cover with a tea towel. Leave in a warm place for 1 hour, or until doubled in size.

3 For the topping, heat the oil in a saucepan over a very low heat. Add the onions, garlic, and herbs. Cover and simmer gently, stirring occasionally, for 1 hour, or until the onions look like a stringy purée. Be careful not to let the onions catch – if they begin to stick, add a little water. Drain well, and set aside, discarding the bay leaf.

4 Preheat the oven to 180°C (350°F/Gas 4). Knead the dough briefly on a floured surface. Roll it out so it is thin and large enough to fit the Swiss roll tin. Prick all over with a fork.

5 Spread the onions over the base. Drain the anchovies, reserving 3 tbsp of oil, and slice the fillets in half lengthways. Embed the olives in the dough, and arrange the anchovies in a criss-cross pattern on top of the onions. Drizzle with the reserved anchovy oil, and sprinkle with pepper.

6 Bake for 25 minutes, or until the crust is brown. The onions should not brown or dry out. Remove and serve warm, or allow to cool. Cut into rectangles, squares, or wedges before serving.

FREEZING INSTRUCTIONS Leave to cool in the tin, then double wrap in cling film and freeze in the tin for up to 1 month. To serve, defrost in the refrigerator overnight, then reheat in a microwave on Medium for 1–2 minutes, turn, and heat for a further 1–2 minutes, or until piping hot. Leave to stand for 5 minutes before serving.

serves 4

**prep 20 mins,
plus rising
• cook 1 hr
25 mins**

**32.5 × 23cm
(13 × 9in)
non-stick
Swiss roll tin**

Pizzette

You could also try your own favourite toppings on these mini party pizzas.

INGREDIENTS
1 quantity basic pizza dough (see page 156)
flour, for dusting
3 tbsp green pesto
3 tbsp sun-dried tomato paste
60g (2oz) sliced salami or pepperoni, cut into strips
6 pitted black olives, halved
60g (2oz) mozzarella, sliced
30g (1oz) wild rocket leaves, chopped
2 tbsp pine nuts
extra virgin olive oil, to drizzle

METHOD
1 Knead the dough on a lightly floured surface, and roll out to about 5mm (¹/₄in) thick. Using a 7.5cm (3in) round biscuit cutter, stamp out 24 rounds, gathering up the dough trimmings and re-rolling as required. Lift on to greased baking trays.

2 Spread half the rounds with green pesto and half with sun-dried tomato paste. Top the pesto rounds with salami or pepperoni, black olives, and mozzarella. Top the sun-dried tomato rounds with wild rocket and pine nuts.

3 Drizzle or brush with the oil, and set aside for 20 minutes, or until risen.

4 Preheat the oven to 220°C (425°F/Gas 7), and bake the pizzettes for 12–15 minutes, or until puffed and golden brown.

FREEZING INSTRUCTIONS Leave to cool completely, then double wrap in cling film and freeze for up to 1 month. To serve, defrost overnight in the refrigerator, then reheat in a microwave on Medium for 1–2 minutes, turn, and heat for a further 1–2 minutes, or until piping hot. Let stand for 5 minutes before serving.

makes 24

prep 20 mins, plus making the dough • cook 12–15 mins

7.5cm (3in) round biscuit cutter

Calzone with peppers, capers, and olives

A calzone is a folded pizza with a filling inside. They are very portable and great for lunch boxes and picnics.

INGREDIENTS
1 quantity basic pizza dough (see page 156)
flour, to dust
semolina, for sprinkling
3–4 ready-roasted peppers from a jar,
   drained and chopped
handful of pitted black olives,
   roughly chopped
1–2 tsp capers, rinsed
2–3 tbsp ricotta cheese or mozzarella,
   torn into pieces
salt and freshly ground black pepper

METHOD
1 Preheat the oven to its highest setting. Very lightly oil a baking tray and put it in the oven to get hot. They both need to be really hot before cooking the calzone.

2 Place the dough on a floured surface and use a rolling pin to roll it out as thinly as you can – about 25–30cm (10–12in) in diameter. Sprinkle the hot baking tray with semolina and transfer the dough on to it.

3 Spoon the peppers, olives, capers, and ricotta cheese or mozzarella on to half the pizza base, leaving about 1cm (1/2in) around the edge. Season well with salt and pepper. Dampen the edges of the pizza with a little water, then fold one half of the pizza over the other, and seal together with your fingers. Sprinkle the top with a little water, then bake for 15–20 minutes, or until golden and crispy.

FREEZING INSTRUCTIONS Leave to cool completely, then double wrap in cling film and freeze for up to 1 month. To serve, defrost overnight in the refrigerator, then reheat in a microwave on Medium for 1–2 minutes, turn, and heat for a further 1–2 minutes, or until piping hot. Leave to stand for 5 minutes before serving.

makes 1

prep 15 mins,
plus making
the dough
• cook 20 mins

Swiss chard and Gruyère cheese tart

With its subtle bitterness, Swiss chard adds character to this cheese tart.

INGREDIENTS

300g (10oz) ready-made shortcrust pastry
flour, for dusting
2 eggs, plus 1 extra, lightly beaten, for egg wash
1 tbsp olive oil
1 onion, finely chopped
salt and freshly ground black pepper
2 garlic cloves, grated or finely chopped
few sprigs of rosemary, leaves picked and finely chopped
250g (9oz) Swiss chard, stalks trimmed and leaves roughly chopped
125g (4^1/$_2$oz) Gruyère cheese, grated
125g (4^1/$_2$oz) feta cheese, cubed
200ml (7fl oz) double cream or whipping cream

METHOD

1 Preheat the oven to 200°C (400°F/Gas 6). Roll out the pastry on a floured work surface and use to line the tart tin. Trim away the excess, line the pastry shell with greaseproof paper, and fill with baking beans. Bake in the oven for 15–30 minutes until the edges are golden. Remove the beans and paper, and brush the bottom of the shell with a little of the egg wash. Return to the oven for 1–2 minutes to crisp. Remove from the oven, and set aside. Reduce the oven temperature to 180°C (350°F/Gas 4).

2 Heat the oil in a pan over a low heat. Add the onion and a pinch of salt, and sweat gently for about 5 minutes until soft and translucent. Add the garlic and rosemary, and cook for a few seconds, then add the Swiss chard. Stir for about 5 minutes until it wilts.

3 Spoon the onion and chard mixture into the pastry shell. Sprinkle over the Gruyère cheese, and scatter evenly with the feta. Season well with salt and pepper. Mix together the cream and the 2 eggs until well combined, and carefully pour over the tart filling. Bake in the oven for 30–40 minutes until set and golden. Leave to cool for 10 minutes before releasing from the tin. Serve warm or at room temperature.

FREEZING INSTRUCTIONS Leave to cool completely, then wrap in greaseproof paper and a double wrapping of cling film and freeze for up to 1 month. To serve, remove the cling film and defrost in the refrigerator overnight. Reheat in an oven preheated to 180°C (350°F) for 30–40 minutes until piping hot (cover with foil if it starts to brown). Alternatively, reheat portions in a microwave on Medium for 2–3 minutes, or until piping hot. Leave to stand for 5 minutes before serving.

serves 6

prep 15 mins, plus cooling • cook 1 hr

23cm (9in) loose-bottomed fluted tart tin • baking beans

Spicy beef pies

Aromatic, tender beef encased in crumbly pastry.

INGREDIENTS

2 tbsp olive oil
250g (9oz) rump steak
1 onion, finely chopped
salt
2 garlic cloves, grated or finely chopped
1–2 green chillies, deseeded and finely chopped
5cm (2in) piece of fresh root ginger,
   peeled and finely chopped

1 tsp coriander seeds, crushed
125g (4$^{1}/_{2}$oz) mushrooms, finely chopped
$^{1}/_{2}$ tsp cayenne pepper
300g (10oz) ready-made shortcrust pastry
flour, for dusting
1 egg, lightly beaten, for egg wash

METHOD

1 Preheat the oven to 200°C (400°F/Gas 6). Heat 1 tbsp of the oil in a large frying pan over a medium-high heat. Add the steak, and brown for about 3 minutes on each side to seal. Remove from the pan, and set aside.

2 Heat the remaining oil in the same pan over a low heat. Add the onion and a pinch of salt, and sweat for about 5 minutes until soft and translucent. Add the garlic, chillies, ginger, and coriander seeds, and cook, stirring, for about 2 minutes until fragrant. Tip in the mushrooms, season with the cayenne, and continue cooking over a low heat for 5 minutes until the mushrooms soften and begin to release their juice.

3 Slice the reserved steak into strips, and return to the pan along with 1 tbsp of water. Cook for about 2 minutes until the mixture is thick and moist, but not too runny.

4 Roll out the pastry on a floured work surface, and cut into 4 squares of 18cm (7in) squares. Wet each square around the edges with a little water. Divide the meat and onion filling into 4 equal portions, and spoon each one into the middle of a square. Bring together the opposite corners of each pastry square to form a parcel, pinching together to seal. Brush all over with the egg wash, and bake in the oven for 20–30 minutes until golden. Serve hot.

FREEZING INSTRUCTIONS Leave to cool completely, then wrap in greaseproof paper and a double wrapping of cling film and freeze for up to 3 months. To serve, remove the cling film and defrost in the refrigerator overnight. Reheat in a microwave on High for 2–3 minutes, turn, and heat for a further 2–3 minutes, or until piping hot. Leave to stand for 5 minutes before serving.

serves 2

prep 20 mins
• cook 50 mins

Olive and anchovy open tart

Storecupboard ingredients make this a perfect dish when time is short.

INGREDIENTS
375g (13oz) ready-made puff pastry
1 egg, lightly beaten, for egg wash
3 tbsp tomato passata
12 unsalted anchovies in oil, drained
12 black olives, pitted
freshly ground black pepper

METHOD
1 Preheat the oven to 200°C (400°F/Gas 6). Roll out the pastry, and lay on a baking tray. Using a sharp knife, score a line about 5cm (2in) in from the edges all the way around to form a border, but do not cut all the way through the pastry. Next, using the back of the knife, score the pastry all the way around the outer edges. This helps it to puff up when cooking.

2 Brush the border with the egg wash, then smooth the passata over the inside area, spreading up to the scored edges. Arrange the anchovies and olives over the tart, and sprinkle over a pinch of pepper.

3 Bake in the oven for about 15 minutes, until the pastry is cooked and the edges are puffed and golden. Cut into 6 squares, and serve warm.

FREEZING INSTRUCTIONS Leave to cool completely, then wrap in greaseproof paper and a double wrapping of cling film and freeze for up to 1 month. To serve, remove the cling film and defrost in the refrigerator overnight. Reheat portions in a microwave on Medium for 3–4 minutes until piping hot. Leave to stand for 5 minutes before serving.

GOOD WITH A crisp green salad.

serves 6

prep 15 mins
• cook 15 mins

Chicken and sweetcorn pie

Creamy and filling with a flaky pastry lid – this pie makes a generous lunch.

INGREDIENTS
2 tbsp olive oil
3 skinless chicken breast fillets, cut into chunks
salt and freshly ground black pepper
1 onion, finely chopped
1 tbsp plain flour, plus extra for dusting
150ml (5fl oz) double cream
300ml (10fl oz) hot vegetable stock
340g can sweetcorn kernels, drained
handful of flat-leaf parsley, finely chopped
300g (10oz) ready-made puff pastry
1 egg, lightly beaten, for egg wash

METHOD
1 Preheat the oven to 200°C (400°F/Gas 6). Heat 1 tbsp of the oil in a large frying pan over a medium-high heat. Season the chicken with salt and pepper. Add to the pan, and cook, stirring, for about 10 minutes until golden brown all over. Remove from the pan, and set aside.

2 Heat the remaining oil in the same pan over a low heat, and add the onion and a pinch of salt. Sweat gently for about 5 minutes until soft and translucent. Remove from the heat, and stir in the flour and a little of the cream. Return the pan to a low heat, and add the remaining cream and the stock, stirring continuously for 5–8 minutes until the mixture thickens. Stir through the sweetcorn and parsley, and season well with salt and pepper.

3 Spoon the mixture into a pie dish or dishes. Roll out the pastry on a floured work surface so that it is 5cm (2in) larger all around than the top of the pie dish. Cut off a strip of pastry about 2.5cm (1in) wide from the edge of the rolled out pastry to make a collar. Wet the edge of the dish with a little water; fit the pastry strip all the way around, and press down firmly. Brush the pastry collar with a little of the egg wash, then top with the pastry lid. Using your fingers or the back of a fork, pinch or press together the edges to seal.

4 Brush the top well with the egg wash. Make 2 slits in the top to allow steam to escape, and bake the pie or pies in the oven for 30–40 minutes until the pastry is puffed and golden. Serve hot.

FREEZING INSTRUCTIONS Leave to cool completely, then wrap in cling film and foil and freeze for up to 3 months. To serve, unwrap and defrost in the refrigerator overnight. Reheat in a microwave on High for 3–4 minutes, rotate the dish, and heat for a further 3–4 minutes, or until piping hot. Leave to stand for 5 minutes before serving.

serves 4

prep 15 mins
• cook 1 hr

1.2-litre (2-pint)
pie dish or
4 individual
pie dishes

175

Lamb and pea pie

Fragrant spiced lamb with crumbly golden shortcrust topping.

INGREDIENTS

1–2 tbsp olive oil

1 onion, finely chopped

salt and freshly ground black pepper

2 garlic cloves, grated or finely chopped

350g (12oz) lamb leg steaks, cut into
   bite-sized pieces

1 tsp ground turmeric

$^1/_2$ tsp ground allspice

2 tbsp plain flour

900ml ($1^1/_2$ pints) hot vegetable stock

2 waxy potatoes, peeled and cut into
   small cubes

125g ($4^1/_2$ oz) frozen peas, thawed

300g (10oz) ready-made shortcrust pastry

1 egg, lightly beaten, for egg wash

METHOD

1 Heat 1 tbsp of the oil in a large pan over a low heat. Add the onion and a pinch of salt, and sweat gently for about 5 minutes until soft and translucent. Add the garlic then increase the heat to medium, and add a little extra oil if needed. Tip in the lamb, and sprinkle over the turmeric and allspice. Cook, stirring now and then, for 6–8 minutes until the lamb is browned all over.

2 Remove from the heat, and stir in the flour and 1 tbsp of the stock. Return to the heat, and pour in the remaining stock. Bring to the boil, reduce the heat to low, and add the potatoes. Simmer gently, stirring occasionally so that the mixture doesn't stick, for about 20 minutes until the potatoes have cooked and the sauce has thickened. Add the peas, and season well with salt and pepper.

3 Meanwhile, preheat the oven to 200°C (400°F/Gas 6). Spoon the meat filling into the pie dish. On a floured work surface, roll out the pastry so that it is about 5cm (2in) larger than the top of the pie dish. Cut out a strip of pastry about 2.5cm (1in) in from the edge to make a collar. Wet the edge of the pie dish with a little water; fit the pastry strip all the way around, and press down firmly. Brush the pastry collar with a little of the egg wash, then top with the pastry lid. Trim away the excess. Using your finger and thumb, pinch together the edges to seal, and decorate the top with any leftover pastry, if you wish.

4 Brush the top of the pie all over with the remaining egg wash. Using a sharp knife, make 2 slits in the top to allow steam to escape. Bake in the oven for 30–40 minutes until cooked and golden all over. Serve hot.

FREEZING INSTRUCTIONS Leave to cool completely, then wrap in cling film and foil and freeze for up to 3 months. To serve, unwrap and defrost in the refrigerator overnight. Reheat in a microwave on High for 3–4 minutes, rotate the dish, and heat for a further 3–4 minutes, or until piping hot. Leave to stand for 5 minutes before serving.

serves 4

**prep 15 mins
• cook 1 hr
15 mins**

**1.2-litre (2-pint)
pie dish**

Fish and leek pie

You can use any white fish for this pie – choose the freshest available.

INGREDIENTS
1 tbsp olive oil
1 onion, finely chopped
salt and freshly ground black pepper
4 leeks, finely sliced
1 tsp plain flour, plus extra for dusting
150ml (5fl oz) cider
handful of flat-leaf parsley, finely chopped
150ml (5fl oz) double cream
675g (1^1/$_2$lb) raw white fish, such as haddock or pollack,
   cut into chunks
300g (10oz) ready-made puff pastry
1 egg, lightly beaten, for egg wash

METHOD
1 Preheat the oven to 200°C (400°F/Gas 6). Heat the oil in a large frying pan over a low heat. Add the onion and a pinch of salt, and sweat gently for about 5 minutes until soft and translucent. Add the leeks, and continue to sweat gently for about 10 minutes until softened. Remove from the heat, stir in the flour, and add a little of the cider. Return to the heat, pour in the remaining cider, and cook for 5–8 minutes until thickened.

2 Stir through the parsley and cream, and spoon the mixture into the pie dish with the fish. Combine gently, and season well with salt and pepper.

3 Roll out the pastry on a floured work surface so that it is about 5cm (2in) larger all around than the top of the pie dish. Cut off a strip of pastry about 2.5cm (1in) wide from the edge of the rolled pastry to make a collar. Wet the edge of the pie dish with a little water; fit the pastry strip all the way around, and press down firmly. Brush the pastry collar with a little of the egg wash, then top with the pastry lid. Trim away the excess, and pinch together the edges to seal. Using a sharp knife, make 2 slits in the top to allow steam to escape.

4 Brush the top of the pie all over with the egg wash, and bake in the oven for 20–30 minutes until the pastry is puffed and golden. Serve hot.

FREEZING INSTRUCTIONS Leave to cool completely, then wrap in cling film and foil and freeze for up to 3 months. To serve, unwrap and defrost in the refrigerator overnight. Reheat in a microwave on High for 3–4 minutes, rotate the dish, and heat for a further 3–4 minutes, or until piping hot. Leave to stand for 5 minutes before serving.

serves 4

prep 15 mins • cook 50 mins

1.2-litre (2-pint) pie dish

Pea and pancetta tart

Frozen peas provide a wonderful sweetness to this salty tart.

INGREDIENTS

300g (10oz) ready-made shortcrust pastry
flour, for dusting
2 eggs, plus 1 extra, lightly beaten, for egg wash
1 tbsp olive oil
1 onion, finely chopped
salt and freshly ground black pepper
125g (4^1/$_2$oz) pancetta, cubed
6 sage leaves, roughly chopped
225g (8oz) frozen peas
150ml (5fl oz) double cream

METHOD

1 Preheat the oven to 200°C (400°F/Gas 6). Roll out the pastry on a floured work surface, and use to line the tart tin. Trim away the excess, line the pastry shell with greaseproof paper, and fill with baking beans. Bake in the oven for 15–20 minutes until the edges of the pastry are golden. Remove the beans and paper, brush the bottom of the shell with a little of the egg wash, and return to the oven for 2–3 minutes to crisp. Remove from the oven, and set aside. Reduce the oven temperature to 180°C (350°F/Gas 4).

2 Meanwhile, heat the oil in a large frying pan over a low heat. Add the onion and a pinch of salt, and sweat gently for about 5 minutes, until soft and translucent. Add the pancetta and sage, increase the heat a little, and cook for 6–8 minutes until the pancetta is golden and crispy. Stir through the peas, and season well with salt and pepper.

3 Spoon the onion and pancetta mixture into the pastry shell, and level the top. Mix together the eggs and cream, season, and carefully pour the mixture over the filling to cover. Bake in the oven for 20–30 minutes until set and golden. Leave to cool for 10 minutes before releasing from the tin. Serve warm.

FREEZING INSTRUCTIONS Leave to cool completely, then wrap in greaseproof paper and a double wrapping of cling film, and freeze for up to 1 month. To serve, remove the cling film and defrost in the refrigerator overnight. Reheat in an oven preheated to 180°C (350°F) for 30–40 minutes until piping hot (cover with foil if it starts to brown). Alternatively, reheat portions in a microwave on Medium for 2–3 minutes, or until piping hot. Leave to stand for 5 minutes before serving.

GOOD WITH Tomato salad.

serves 4–6

prep 10 mins,
plus cooling
• cook 1 hr
15 mins

18cm (7in) round
loose-bottomed
straight-sided
tart tin
• baking beans

Cheese and onion pie

Tangy Cheddar cheese perfectly complements onion to make this a mouth-watering pie.

INGREDIENTS

1 tbsp olive oil
1 large onion, finely chopped
salt and freshly ground black pepper
2 eggs
200g (7oz) mature Cheddar cheese, grated
350g (12oz) ready-made shortcrust pastry
flour, for dusting

METHOD

1 Preheat the oven to 200°C (400°F/Gas 6). Heat the oil in a small pan over a low heat. Add the onion and a pinch of salt, and sweat for a couple of minutes until transparent and just starting to soften. Tip into a bowl, and leave to cool completely. Lightly beat one of the eggs, and stir into the cooled onion with the cheese. Season with salt and pepper.

2 Halve the pastry, and roll out each piece on a floured work surface. Use one of the pastry circles to line the pie tin, overlapping the edges, and fill with the cheese and onion mixture. Wet the edge of the pastry with a little water, then top with the other round of pastry. Trim away the excess, then pinch the edges together with your finger and thumb to seal. Using a sharp knife, make two slits in the top of the pie to allow steam to escape.

3 Lightly beat the remaining egg to make an egg wash, and brush all over the top of the pie. Bake in the oven for 25–35 minutes until cooked and golden.

FREEZING INSTRUCTIONS Leave to cool completely, then wrap in greaseproof paper and a double wrapping of plastic wrap and freeze for up to 3 months. To serve, remove the cling film and defrost in the refrigerator overnight. Reheat portions in a microwave on Medium for 2–3 minutes, turn, and heat for a further 2–3 minutes, or until piping hot. Leave to stand for 5 minutes before serving.

GOOD WITH A mixed salad and boiled or steamed new potatoes.

serves 4

prep 15 mins,
plus cooling
• cook 40 mins

18cm (7in)
round pie tin

Mushroom and ricotta pies with red pepper pesto

To prevent damp pastry, leave the sides slightly open to allow steam to escape.

INGREDIENTS
120ml (4fl oz) olive oil
300g (10oz) button mushrooms, halved
1 leek, white part only, finely sliced
2 sheets ready-rolled puff pastry (preferably made with butter), thawed if frozen
200g (7oz) ricotta cheese
1 egg yolk, lightly beaten

For the red pepper pesto
2 tbsp olive oil
1 onion, sliced
2 red peppers, sliced
2 garlic cloves, crushed
grated zest and juice of 1 small lemon
salt and freshly ground black pepper

METHOD
1 Preheat the oven to 200°C (400°F/Gas 6), and line a baking tray with baking parchment. To make the red pepper pesto, heat the oil in a heavy frying pan over a low heat. Add the onion, and sweat gently for a few minutes until soft and translucent. Tip in the peppers, and sweat for a further 10–15 minutes until soft. Transfer the onion mixture to a blender or food processor. Add the garlic and lemon zest and juice, and blend to a chunky purée. Season with salt and pepper and set aside.

2 Heat another 3 tbsp of the oil in a clean large heavy frying pan over a medium heat. Add the mushrooms and leeks, and sauté, stirring, for 5 minutes until the mushrooms have browned. Set aside.

3 Cut each pastry sheet into 4 squares. Using a sharp knife, cut diagonal slashes across the surface of 4 of the pastry squares, being careful not to slice all the way through. Spread the ricotta over the surface of the uncut pastry squares, leaving a 1cm (½ in) border of pastry all around the edges. Spoon the mushroom and leek mixture evenly over the ricotta, then lay the slit pastry squares evenly over the top of the mushrooms. Pinch and twist together the corners of the pies, and brush the tops with the egg yolk.

4 Sit the pies on top of the prepared baking tray, and bake in the oven for about 25 minutes until golden brown. Serve with the red pepper pesto.

FREEZING INSTRUCTIONS Leave to cool completely, then wrap in greasproof paper and a double wrapping of cling film, and freeze for up to 1 month. To serve, remove the cling film and defrost in the refrigerator overnight. Reheat in a microwave on Medium for 3–4 minutes until piping hot. Leave to stand for 5 minutes before serving. The pesto can be kept in the refrigerator topped up with oil for up to 2 weeks.

GOOD WITH A leafy green salad.

serves 4

**prep 25 mins
• cook 45 mins**

**blender or
food processor**

Curried vegetable pies

These individual pies make a convenient and tasty snack.

INGREDIENTS

2 carrots, peeled and diced
2 potatoes, peeled and finely diced
450g (1lb) ready-made shortcrust pastry
flour, for dusting
1 egg, lightly beaten, for egg wash
1 tbsp curry paste
2 tbsp Greek-style yogurt
1 garlic clove, grated or finely chopped
2cm ($^3/_4$in) piece of fresh root ginger, finely chopped
2 spring onions, finely sliced
handful of coriander leaves, finely chopped
juice of $^1/_2$ lemon
salt and freshly ground black pepper

METHOD

1 Preheat the oven to 200°C (400°F/Gas 6). Cook the carrots and potato in a pan of salted water for about 15 minutes until soft; drain well.

2 Roll out the pastry on a floured work surface, then cut out 4 circles using the biscuit cutter. Put the pastry rounds on a baking tray, and brush the edges with a little of the egg wash.

3 Put the carrots and potatoes in a bowl, and gently mix with the curry paste and yogurt. Add the garlic, ginger, spring onions, coriander, and lemon juice, and season well with salt and pepper. Stir through gently until well mixed.

4 Divide the vegetable mixture evenly among the pastry circles, spooning it into the centre of each one. Fold over the pastry to make a half-moon shape, and pinch the edges together to seal. Using a sharp knife, make 2 slashes in the top of each pie, then brush all over with the remaining egg wash. Bake in the oven for 20–30 minutes until golden. Serve hot or cold.

FREEZING INSTRUCTIONS Leave to cool completely, then wrap in greaseproof paper and a double wrapping of cling film, and freeze for up to 3 months. To serve, remove the cling film and defrost in the refrigerator overnight. Reheat in a microwave on Medium for 3–4 minutes, or until piping hot. Leave to stand for 5 minutes before serving.

serves 2

prep 15 mins
• cook 45 mins

15cm (6in) round
biscuit cutter

Gruyère, potato, and thyme tartlets

These individual tartlets are ideal for a light lunch.

INGREDIENTS

300g (10oz) ready-made shortcrust pastry
flour, for dusting.
2 eggs, plus 1 extra, lightly beaten, for egg wash
2 potatoes, peeled and diced into 1cm ($\frac{1}{2}$in) pieces
2 tbsp olive oil
1 small onion, very finely diced
salt and freshly ground black pepper
few sprigs of thyme, leaves picked
150g (5$\frac{1}{2}$oz) Gruyère cheese, grated
200ml (7fl oz) double cream

METHOD

1 Preheat the oven to 200°C (400°F/Gas 6). Roll out the pastry on a floured work surface, and use to line the 4 tart tins. Trim away the excess, line the pastry shells with greaseproof paper, and fill with baking beans. Bake in the oven for 15–20 minutes until the edges are golden. Remove the beans and paper, brush the bottom of each pastry shell with a little of the egg wash, and return to the oven for 2–3 minutes to crisp. Remove from the oven, and set aside. Reduce the oven temperature to 180°C (350°F/Gas 4).

2 Parboil the potatoes in a small pan of water for about 5 minutes until just starting to soften; do not overcook. Drain.

3 Meanwhile, heat the oil in a large non-stick frying pan over a low heat. Add the onion and a pinch of salt, and sweat gently for about 5 minutes until soft and translucent. Add the parboiled potatoes and the thyme, and season with some pepper. Cook, stirring occasionally, for about 10 minutes until the potatoes begin to brown.

4 Remove from the heat, and stir through the Gruyère cheese. Taste, and adjust the seasoning if necessary. Divide the mixture evenly among the pastry shells. Mix together the cream and the 2 eggs, then carefully pour equal amounts into each tart. Sit the tarts on a baking tray, and bake in the oven for 20–30 minutes until set and golden. Serve hot.

FREEZING INSTRUCTIONS Leave to cool completely, then wrap in greaseproof paper and a double layer of cling film, and freeze for up to 1 month. To serve, remove the cling film and defrost in the refrigerator overnight. Reheat in a microwave on Medium for 1–2 minutes, rotate the tarts, and heat for a further 1–2 minutes, or until piping hot. Let stand for 5 minutes before serving.

serves 4

prep 20 mins
• cook 1 hr

4 tart tins,
10cm (4in)
• baking beans

Mixed mushroom and walnut tart

Exotic mushrooms will give this vegetarian tart a fuller flavour.

INGREDIENTS

250g (9oz) ready-made shortcrust pastry
flour, for dusting
2 eggs, plus 1 extra, lightly beaten, for egg wash
3–4 tbsp olive oil
140g (5oz) exotic mushrooms (such as porcini or shiitake),
 roughly chopped
200g (7oz) chestnut mushrooms, roughly chopped
3 garlic cloves, grated or finely chopped
50g (1³/₄oz) walnut halves, roughly chopped
salt and freshly ground black pepper
2 handfuls of spinach leaves, roughly chopped
200ml (7fl oz) double cream

METHOD

1 Preheat the oven to 200°C (400°F/Gas 6). Roll out the pastry on a floured work surface, and use to line the tart tin. Trim away the excess, line the pastry shell with greaseproof paper, and fill with baking beans. Bake in the oven for 15–20 minutes until the edges are golden. Remove the beans and paper, brush the bottom of the shell with a little of the egg wash, and return to the oven for 2–3 minutes to crisp. Remove from the oven, and set aside. Reduce the oven temperature to 180°C (350°F/Gas 4).

2 Heat the oil in a large deep-sided frying pan over a low heat. Add the mushrooms, garlic, and walnuts, and season well with salt and pepper. Cook, stirring occasionally, for about 10 minutes until the mushrooms release their juices. Tip in the spinach, and cook, stirring, for a further 5 minutes until just wilted. Spoon the mixture into the pastry shell.

3 Mix together the cream and the 2 eggs. Season well with salt and pepper. Carefully pour the cream mixture over the mushroom filling. Sprinkle with a pinch of pepper, and bake in the oven for 15–20 minutes until set. Leave to cool for 10 minutes before releasing from the tin. Serve hot or cold.

FREEZING INSTRUCTIONS Leave to cool completely, then wrap in greaseproof paper and a double wrapping of cling film, and freeze for up to 1 month. To serve, remove the cling film and defrost in the refrigerator overnight. Reheat portions in a microwave on Medium for 1–2 minutes, turn, then heat for a further 1–2 minutes, or until piping hot. Leave to stand for 5 minutes before serving. Alternatively, reheat in an oven preheated to 180°C (350°F) for 30 minutes until piping hot (cover with foil if it starts to brown).

serves 6

prep 15 mins,
plus cooling
• cook 1 hr

12 x 35cm
(5 x 14in)
rectangular
loose-bottomed
fluted tart tin
• baking beans

SAUCES

Beef ragù

Easy and versatile, the ragù is a meat-based sauce that goes well with pasta, rice, or potatoes. This beef version will make an excellent staple for your freezer.

INGREDIENTS

4 tbsp olive oil
2 large onions, finely diced
675g (1½lb) lean beef, cut into 1cm (½in) cubes
8 garlic cloves, grated or finely chopped
300ml (10fl oz) red wine
4 x 400g cans chopped tomatoes
2 bay leaves
1 tsp thyme leaves, finely chopped
salt and freshly ground black pepper

METHOD

1 Heat the oil in a large heavy-based pan, add the onions, and cook over a medium heat, stirring frequently, for 5 minutes, or until soft and translucent. Add the beef and cook, stirring frequently, for 5 minutes, or until no longer pink. Add the garlic and cook for 1 minute, then pour in the wine and allow to simmer and reduce for 5 minutes.

2 Add the tomatoes, bay leaves, and thyme, bring to the boil, then reduce the heat and simmer for 30 minutes, stirring occasionally. Taste and season with salt and pepper. Serve hot.

FREEZING INSTRUCTIONS Leave to cool completely, then remove and discard the bay leaves. Divide the ragù evenly among sealable freezer bags (no more than 2 portions per bag) and freeze for up to 6 months. To serve, defrost in the refrigerator overnight, then reheat in a pan. Simmer gently for 15–20 minutes, adding hot water if needed, or until piping hot.

GOOD WITH Pasta or creamy mashed potato.

serves 8

prep 20 mins
• cook 45 mins

194

Lamb and aubergine ragù

Using lean lamb for this recipe will help the meat keep well in the freezer.

INGREDIENTS

6 tbsp olive oil
2 onions, finely diced
2 medium aubergines, cut into 1cm ($^1/_2$in) cubes
450g (1lb) lean lamb, cut into 1cm ($^1/_2$in) cubes
6 garlic cloves, finely chopped
3 x 400g cans chopped tomatoes
3 bay leaves
1 tbsp dried oregano
handful of flat-leaf parsley, chopped
salt and freshly ground black pepper

METHOD

1 Heat the oil in a large heavy-based pan, add the onions, and cook over a medium heat, stirring frequently, for 3 minutes. Add the aubergines and cook, stirring frequently, for 5 minutes, or until starting to brown. Add the lamb, combine well, and cook, stirring frequently, for 5 minutes, or until no longer pink.

2 Stir in the garlic and cook for 1 minute. Add the tomatoes, bay leaves, oregano, and parsley, bring to the boil, then reduce the heat and simmer for 20 minutes, stirring occasionally. Taste, and season with salt and pepper. Serve hot.

FREEZING INSTRUCTIONS Leave to cool completely, then remove and discard the bay leaves. Divide the ragù evenly among sealable freezer bags (no more than 2 portions per bag), ensuring the meat is well covered by the sauce, and freeze for up to 3 months. To serve, defrost in the refrigerator overnight, then reheat in a pan. Simmer gently for 15–20 minutes, adding hot water if needed, or until piping hot.

GOOD WITH Pasta or rice.

serves 8

prep 20 mins
• cook 35 mins

Ragù of venison with wild mushrooms

Slow simmering concentrates the rich flavours of the venison and mushrooms.

INGREDIENTS

1 tbsp olive oil
15g (½oz) butter
4 shallots, sliced
115g (4oz) smoked bacon, diced
600g (1lb 5oz) venison, diced
1 tbsp plain flour
3 tbsp brandy
250g (9oz) wild mushrooms, sliced
250ml (9fl oz) beef stock
1 tbsp tomato purée
1 tbsp Worcestershire sauce
1 tsp dried oregano
salt and freshly ground black pepper

METHOD

1 Heat the oil and butter in the casserole and fry the shallots and bacon over a medium-high heat, stirring frequently, until beginning to brown.

2 Add the venison and fry for 3–4 minutes, or until browned on all sides, stirring frequently. Stir in the flour, then cook for 1–2 minutes, or until beginning to brown.

3 Add the brandy and stir for 30 seconds, then add the mushrooms and stock. Bring to the boil, stirring often.

4 Stir in the tomato purée, Worcestershire sauce, and oregano, and season to taste with salt and pepper. Reduce the heat to low, cover tightly with a lid, and simmer very gently for 1½–2 hours, or until the venison is tender (the cooking time will depend on the age of the meat).

FREEZING INSTRUCTIONS Leave to cool completely, then transfer to a sealable freezerproof container or divide evenly among sealable freezer bags (no more than 2 portions per bag), making sure the meat is well covered by the sauce. Freeze for up to 3 months. To serve, defrost in the refrigerator overnight, then reheat in a pan. Simmer gently for 15–20 minutes, adding hot water or hot stock if needed, or until piping hot.

GOOD WITH Pasta, boiled rice, or potatoes.

serves 4

prep 15 mins
• cook 1½–2 hrs

flameproof
casserole

Rich tomato sauce

Great whether eaten on its own with pasta or used in other recipes, this sauce is so useful that it won't stay in the freezer for long!

INGREDIENTS
4 tbsp olive oil
4 garlic cloves, finely sliced
4 x 400g cans whole tomatoes, chopped in the can
2 tbsp tomato purée
2 tsp dried oregano
2 bay leaves
salt and freshly ground black pepper
2 heaped tsp green pesto

METHOD
1 Heat the oil in a large heavy-based pan, add the garlic, and cook over a low heat for a few seconds. Add the tomatoes and tomato purée, bring to the boil, then add the oregano and bay leaves and simmer for 25 minutes, stirring occasionally.

2 Season well with salt and pepper, cook for 2 minutes, then stir in the pesto and remove from the heat.

FREEZING INSTRUCTIONS Leave to cool completely, then remove and discard the bay leaves. Divide the sauce evenly among sealable freezer bags (no more than 2 portions per bag) and freeze for up to 6 months. To serve, defrost in the refrigerator overnight, then reheat in a pan. Simmer gently for 15–20 minutes, adding hot water if needed, or until piping hot.

GOOD WITH Pasta or use to make a lasagne or moussaka.

serves 8

prep 10 mins
• cook 30 mins

healthy option

Spinach sauce

This is a lovely alternative to a tomato-based sauce.

INGREDIENTS
4 tbsp olive oil
2 large onions, finely diced
4 garlic cloves, finely sliced
2 red chillies, deseeded and finely chopped
550g (1¼lb) baby spinach leaves, rinsed and roughly chopped
300ml (10fl oz) dry white wine
2 tbsp plain flour
900ml (1½ pints) milk
salt and freshly ground black pepper

METHOD
1 Heat the oil in a large heavy-based pan, add the onions, and cook over a medium heat, stirring frequently, for 5 minutes, or until soft and translucent. Stir in the garlic and chillies and cook for 2 minutes. Add the spinach and cook for 3 minutes, or until wilted.

2 Add the wine and simmer for 5 minutes, or until reduced by half. Add the flour and combine well. Pour in half the milk, and stir well. Add the rest of the milk a little at a time, stirring constantly, and cook for 5 minutes, or until you have a creamy sauce. Season well with salt and pepper.

FREEZING INSTRUCTIONS Leave to cool completely, then divide the sauce evenly among sealable freezer bags (no more than 2 portions per bag) and freeze for up to 3 months. To serve, defrost in the refrigerator overnight, then transfer to a pan with a little milk. Heat through gently until hot (but do not overcook).

GOOD WITH Chicken, fish, or new potatoes, or stir in some grated Cheddar cheese and serve with pasta.

serves 8

**prep 15 mins
• cook 20 mins**

healthy option

INSTANT DESSERTS

Make ice cream

Ice cream can be easily made by hand, or with a machine for a finer texture. You can add puréed fruit, nuts, or other flavours to create your own variations.

By hand

1 Split 2 vanilla pods, and scrape out and reserve the seeds. Add the pods to a pan with 500ml (16fl oz) double cream, and bring to the boil. Add 75g (2¹/₂oz) golden caster sugar, and stir until dissolved.

2 In a bowl, whisk 4 egg yolks until well combined, then strain the warm cream mixture into the eggs, stirring all the time. Add the reserved vanilla seeds, and stir.

3 Pour the ice cream mixture into a metal loaf tin or plastic tub. Leave it to cool completely.

4 Once cool, put the container into the freezer. When frozen, double-wrap with cling film and freeze for up to 3 months.

With an ice cream machine

1 Prepare a custard (see steps 1 and 2, opposite) then cool it in a bowl set in a large bowl of ice. Stir continuously to prevent a skin from forming.

2 Pour the custard mixture into an ice cream machine and process until thick and smooth. Place in a freezerproof container and freeze until firm.

Make granita

Combine sugar, fruit juice, and water (or red or white wine) to make a syrup that can be frozen to create a light and refreshing dessert.

1 Slowly bring the ingredients to the boil, reduce the heat, and simmer for 2–3 minutes, stirring. Cool, pour into a shallow baking tray, and freeze. When half-frozen, use a fork to break up the chunks.

2 Break up the crystals once or twice more until evenly frozen. Remove from the freezer 5–10 minutes before serving, to thaw slightly. Scrape up the frozen granita and serve in pre-chilled glasses.

Vanilla ice cream

Nothing beats creamy home-made vanilla ice cream – you'll keep coming back for more.

INGREDIENTS

1 vanilla pod
300ml (10fl oz) milk
3 egg yolks
85g (3oz) caster sugar
300ml (10fl oz) double cream

METHOD

1 Split the vanilla pod, scrape out the seeds, and put the seeds, vanilla pod, and milk into a heavy saucepan and bring almost to the boil. Remove from the heat, cover, and set aside for 30 minutes.

2 Beat the egg yolks and sugar in a large bowl. Stir in the infused milk then strain back into the pan. Cook the mixture over a low heat, stirring constantly, until the mixture thickens slightly and just coats the back of a spoon. Do not boil the mixture or the custard will curdle. Pour the mixture back into the bowl and cool completely.

3 Whisk the cream into the cooled custard. To freeze the ice cream by hand, pour the mixture into a freezerproof container and freeze for at least 3–4 hours, then whisk to break up any ice crystals. Freeze for a further 2 hours and repeat the process, then freeze until ready to use. To freeze using an ice cream machine, pour the mixture into the prepared freezer bowl and churn according to the manufacturer's instructions. This should take 20–30 minutes. Transfer to a freezerproof container and freeze until needed.

FREEZING INSTRUCTIONS Freeze for up to 3 months. To serve the ice cream, remove it from the freezer 20–30 minutes prior to scooping.

serves 4

prep 25 mins, plus cooling and freezing • cook 12 mins

allow at least 6 hrs for freezing

ice cream machine desirable

Strawberry semifreddo

This is Italian ice cream with a twist; texture and sweetness
are added by crushed meringues.

INGREDIENTS
225g (8oz) strawberries, hulled, plus extra whole
    strawberries and redcurrants to decorate
250ml (9fl oz) double cream
50g (1³/₄oz) icing sugar
115g (4oz) ready-made meringues, coarsely crushed
3 tbsp raspberry-flavoured liqueur

For the coulis
225g (8oz) strawberries, hulled
25–50g (1–1³/₄oz) icing sugar
1–2 tsp lemon juice, brandy, grappa, or balsamic vinegar

METHOD
1 Lightly brush the tin with vegetable oil, line the base with greaseproof paper, and set aside.

2 Purée the strawberries in a blender or food processor. Whip the cream with the icing sugar just until it holds its shape. Fold the strawberry purée and cream together, then fold in the crushed meringues and liqueur. Turn the mixture into the tin, smooth the surface, cover with cling film, and freeze for at least 6 hours or overnight if possible.

3 Meanwhile, make the strawberry coulis. Purée the strawberries in a blender or food processor, then press them through a fine sieve to remove the seeds. Stir 25g (scant 1oz) icing sugar into the purée and taste for sweetness, adding more sugar if you like it sweet. Flavour the coulis with the lemon juice, or other flavouring listed above.

4 Just before serving, remove the semifreddo from the tin, peel away the lining paper, and using a warmed knife, cut into slices. Arrange the slices on individual plates, spoon the coulis around the base, and decorate with whole strawberries and redcurrants.

FREEZING INSTRUCTIONS Freeze the semifreddo for up to 3 months. Do not freeze the coulis but make it on the day you wish to serve the semifreddo.

serves 6–8

prep 20 mins,
plus freezing

freeze for at
least 6 hrs, or
overnight if
possible

20cm (8in)
loose-bottomed
springform tin
• blender or
food processor

Double chocolate ice cream

White chocolate chips set in dark chocolate ice cream makes this dessert a double chocolate heaven.

INGREDIENTS

1 vanilla pod
300ml (10fl oz) milk
125g (4$^{1}/_{2}$oz) dark chocolate, roughly chopped
3 egg yolks
85g (3oz) caster sugar
300ml (10fl oz) double cream
175g (6oz) white chocolate chips

METHOD

1 Split the vanilla pod, scrape out the seeds, and place both into a heavy pan over a low heat with the milk. Add the dark chocolate and stir gently until it has melted. Bring almost to the boil, then remove from the heat, cover, and set aside for 20 minutes.

2 Beat the egg yolks and sugar together in a large bowl. Stir in the infused milk, then strain the mixture back into the saucepan. Discard the vanilla pod. Cook the mixture over a low heat, stirring constantly until it thickens slightly and coats the back of a spoon. It is important that the mixture does not boil, or it will curdle. Pour the thickened mixture into a bowl and let it cool completely.

3 When the mixture is cool, whisk in the cream. To freeze the ice cream by hand, pour the mixture into a freezerproof container and freeze for at least 3–4 hours, then stir. Freeze for a further 2 hours and stir again. Stir in the white chocolate chips and freeze until ready to use. To freeze the ice cream in an ice cream machine, pour in the mixture and churn according to the manufacturer's instructions. This should take about 20–30 minutes. Transfer to a freezerproof container and freeze until ready to serve.

FREEZING INSTRUCTIONS Freeze for up to 3 months. To serve, remove the ice cream from the freezer 10–15 minutes before scooping.

serves 4

prep 25 mins,
plus cooling
and freezing
• cook 12 mins

allow at
least 5–6 hrs
for freezing

ice cream
machine
desirable

Pistachio ice cream

The seed of an Asian tree, the pistachio nut has a hard outer shell with a distinctive soft green nutty centre.

INGREDIENTS

300ml (10fl oz) milk
1/2 tsp almond extract
3 egg yolks
85g (3oz) caster sugar
few drops of green food colouring (optional)
175g (6oz) pistachio nuts, shelled and
   roughly chopped, plus extra to decorate
300ml (10fl oz) double cream, lightly whipped

METHOD

1 Heat the milk in a heavy saucepan and bring almost to the boil. Stir in the almond extract.

2 Beat the egg yolks and sugar in a large bowl until creamy. Stir in the milk, then strain back into the saucepan. Cook the mixture over a low heat, stirring constantly, until the mixture thickens slightly, or just coats the back of a spoon. Do not boil the mixture or the custard will curdle.

3 Pour back into the bowl, stir in the food colouring, if using, and the pistachio nuts, and allow to cool completely. Fold the cream into the cooled custard.

4 To freeze the ice cream by hand, pour the mixture into a freezerproof container and freeze for 3–4 hours, then use a fork to break up any ice crystals. Freeze for a further 2 hours and repeat the process. Freeze until ready to serve. To freeze the ice cream in an ice cream machine, pour in the mixture and churn according to the manufacturer's instructions. This should take about 20–30 minutes. Transfer to a freezerproof container and freeze until ready to serve.

FREEZING INSTRUCTIONS Freeze for up to 3 months. Remove the ice cream from the freezer 15 minutes prior to serving. Serve the scoops scattered with chopped pistachios.

serves 4

prep 25–30 mins,
plus cooling
and freezing
• cook
12–15 mins

allow at least
6 hrs for freezing

ice cream
machine
desirable

Orange sorbet

Juice-based sorbets are often served in restaurants between courses as a refreshing palate cleanser. They also make a lovely, light summer dessert.

INGREDIENTS

2 large oranges
125g (4$^1\!/_2$oz) caster sugar
1 tbsp orange-flower water
1 egg white

METHOD

1 Using a vegetable peeler, pare the zest from the oranges, taking care not to include the pith. Place the sugar and 300ml (10fl oz) water into a pan and heat gently until the sugar has dissolved. Add the orange zest and simmer gently for 10 minutes. Allow to cool slightly.

2 Squeeze the juice from the oranges, and add to the sugar mixture. To gain as much juice from your fruit as possible, warm it slightly by rolling it between your hands, or on a work surface, before squeezing.

3 Stir the orange-flower water into the orange syrup, then strain into a shallow container. In a separate, very clean bowl, whisk the egg white to soft peaks, then fold into the orange mixture.

4 If you do not have an ice cream machine, pour the mixture into a freezerproof container and freeze for at least 4 hours, or until almost frozen solid. Mash the mixture with a fork to break up any ice crystals, then freeze until solid. If using an ice cream machine, pour the mixture into the freezer compartment, and churn according to the manufacturer's instructions. Transfer to a freezerproof container and freeze until ready to use.

FREEZING INSTRUCTIONS Freeze for up to 3 months. Remove the sorbet from the freezer 15–30 minutes before serving to allow it to soften slightly.

serves 4

prep 10 mins, plus freezing • cook 15 mins

allow at least 4 hrs for freezing

ice cream machine desirable

Zesty lemon granita

Although Italians often eat this on its own as a refreshing sweet treat on a hot day, it makes a delicious dessert after a rich main course.

INGREDIENTS
6 lemons
115g (4oz) caster sugar
twists of lemon zest, to decorate

METHOD
1 Set the freezer to its coldest setting and place freezerproof serving bowls or glasses in the freezer. Using a cannelle knife or lemon zester with a v-shaped cutter, thinly pare the zest from 4 of the lemons, and set aside, then grate the zest from the remaining 2 lemons, and set aside, separately.

2 Dissolve the sugar in 250ml (9fl oz) of water in a small pan over a medium heat. Increase the heat and bring to the boil, then boil for 5 minutes, or until it turns to a light syrup.

3 Pour the syrup into a shallow, freezerproof non-metallic bowl. Stir in the pared lemon zest and set aside to cool completely.

4 Meanwhile, squeeze the lemons to make about 250ml (9fl oz) of lemon juice. Remove the pared lemon zest strips from the mixture. Stir in the lemon juice and grated zest.

5 Transfer to the freezer for 1–2 hours, or until frozen around the edges and still slightly slushy in the middle. Every 30 minutes or so, use a fork to break up the frozen granita. Continue for 4 hours, or until the mixture has the texture of shaved ice, then leave the granita in the freezer until ready to serve. (See step-by-step technique on page 207).

FREEZING INSTRUCTIONS Freeze for up to 1 month. Serve straight from the freezer.

GOOD WITH A small sweet biscuit.

serves 4

prep 5–10 mins,
plus cooling
and freezing
• cook 5 mins

allow at least
4 hrs for freezing

shallow,
freezerproof
non-metallic
bowl

Espresso granita

The texture of granita should be crystallized, like shaved ice. Although light, this dessert has a delightfully heady character.

INGREDIENTS

100g (3^1/$_2$oz) caster sugar
^{1}/$_2$ tsp pure vanilla extract
300ml (10fl oz) very strong espresso coffee, chilled

METHOD

1 Set the freezer to its coldest setting and place freezerproof serving bowls or glasses in the freezer. Dissolve the sugar in 300ml (10fl oz) water in a small saucepan over a medium heat. Increase the heat and bring to the boil, then boil for 5 minutes to make a light syrup.

2 Pour the syrup into a shallow, freezerproof dish. Stir in the vanilla and coffee and set aside to cool completely.

3 Transfer to the freezer. Every 30 minutes or so, use a fork to break up the frozen chunks. Continue to do this for 4 hours, or until the mixture has the texture of shaved ice, then leave the granita in the freezer until ready to serve. (See step-by-step technique on page 207.)

FREEZING INSTRUCTIONS Freeze for up to 1 month. Serve straight from the freezer.

serves 4

prep 5 mins, plus cooling and freezing • cook 5 mins

allow at least 4 hrs for freezing

SCOTTISH BORDERS COUNCIL

LIBRARY &

INFORMATION SERVICES

INDEX

Page numbers in *italics* indicate illustrations.

Useful information

Refrigerator and freezer storage guidelines

FOOD	REFRIGERATOR	FREEZER
Raw poultry, fish, and meat (small pieces)	2–3 days	3 months
Raw minced beef and poultry	1–3 days	3 months
Cooked whole roasts or whole poultry	2–3 days	9 months
Cooked poultry pieces	2–3 days	3 months
Soups and stocks	2–3 days	3–6 months
Stews	2–3 days	3 months
Pies	2–3 days	3–6 months

Oven temperature equivalents

CELSIUS	FAHRENHEIT	GAS	DESCRIPTION
110°C	225°F	$1/4$	Cool
130°C	250°F	$1/2$	Cool
140°C	275°F	1	Very low
150°C	300°F	2	Very low
160°C	325°F	3	Low
180°C	350°F	4	Moderate
190°C	375°F	5	Moderately hot
200°C	400°F	6	Hot
220°C	425°F	7	Hot
230°C	450°F	8	Very hot
240°C	475°F	9	Very hot